C000205859

EA[ST] AN[G] Regional [Road] Atlas

CONTENTS

REFERENCE

MOTORWAY	M1
Under Construction	
Proposed	
MOTORWAY JUNCTIONS WITH NUMBERS	4
Unlimited interchange	4
Limited interchange	8
MOTORWAY SERVICE AREA	FERRYBRIDGE (S)
MAJOR ROAD SERVICE AREAS with 24 hour Facilities	LEEMING (S) GRASBY (S)
PRIMARY ROUTE	A19
PRIMARY ROUTE DESTINATION	DOVER
DUAL CARRIAGEWAY (A & B Roads)	
CLASS A ROAD	A614
CLASS B ROAD	B6422
MAJOR ROAD UNDER CONSTRUCTION	
MAJOR ROAD PROPOSED	
GRADIENT 1:5(20%) & STEEPER (Ascent in direction of arrow)	«
TOLL	TOLL
MILEAGE BETWEEN MARKERS	8
RAILWAY AND STATION	
LEVEL CROSSING AND TUNNEL	
RIVER OR CANAL	
COUNTY BOUNDARY	
BUILT UP AREA	
VILLAGE OR HAMLET	
WOODED AREA	
SPOT HEIGHT IN FEET	• 813
HEIGHT ABOVE SEA LEVEL 400' - 1,000' 1,000' - 1,400' 1,400' - 2,000' 2,000' +	
NATIONAL GRID REFERENCE (Kilometres)	100

TOURIST INFORMATION

AIRPORT	✈
AIRFIELD	✈
HELIPORT	
BATTLE SITE AND DATE	⚔ 1408
CASTLE (Open to Public)	
CASTLE WITH GARDEN (Open to Public)	
CATHEDRAL, ABBEY, FRIARY, PRIORY, CHURCH (Open to Public)	✝
COUNTRY PARK	
FERRY (Vehicular) __ 🚢 🚣 (Foot only)	
GARDEN (Open to Public)	
GOLF COURSE __ 9 HOLE __ ⛳ 18 HOLE __	
HISTORIC BUILDING (Open to Public)	
HISTORIC BUILDING WITH GARDEN (Open to Public)	
HORSE RACECOURSE	
INFORMATION CENTRE, VISITOR CENTRE OR TOURIST INFORMATION CENTRE	🅸
LIGHTHOUSE	
MOTOR RACING CIRCUIT	
MUSEUM, ART GALLERY	
NATIONAL PARK OR FOREST PARK	
NATIONAL TRUST PROPERTY (Open)	NT
(Restricted Opening)	NT
NATURE RESERVE OR BIRD SANCTUARY	
NATURE TRAIL OR FOREST WALK	
PLACE OF INTEREST _____ Monument •	
PICNIC SITE	
RAILWAY (Preserved, Miniature, Steam or Narrow Gauge)	
TELEPHONE __ PUBLIC (Selection) __ ☎ AA OR RAC __	☏
THEME PARK	
VIEWPOINT	
WILDLIFE PARK	
WINDMILL	
ZOO OR SAFARI PARK	

SCALE

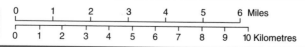

1:158,400
2.5 Miles to 1 Inch

Geographers' A-Z Map Company Ltd

Head Office : Fairfield Road,
Borough Green, Sevenoaks, Kent TN15 8PP
Telephone : 01732- 781000
Showrooms :
44 Gray's Inn Road, London, WC1X 8HX
Telephone 0171-242 9246

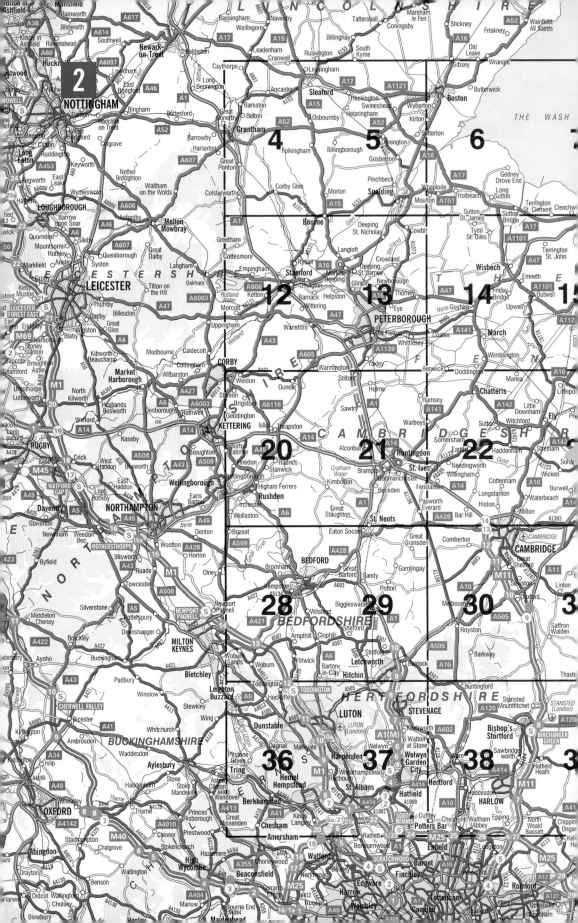

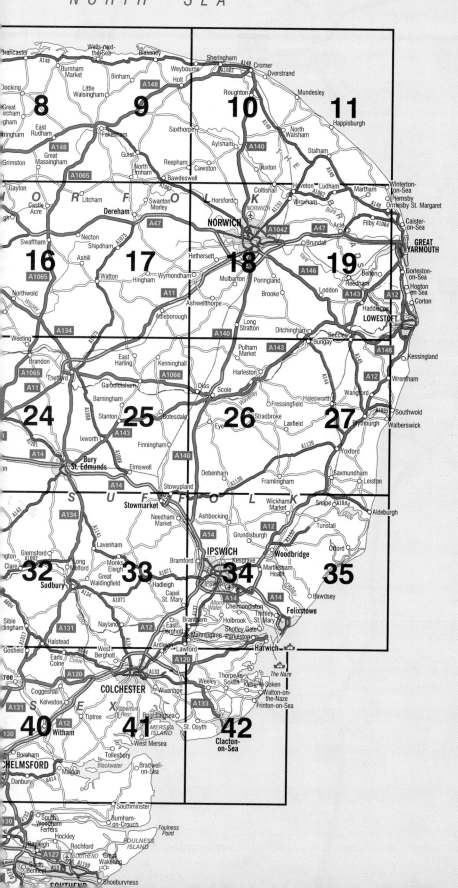

NORTH SEA

3

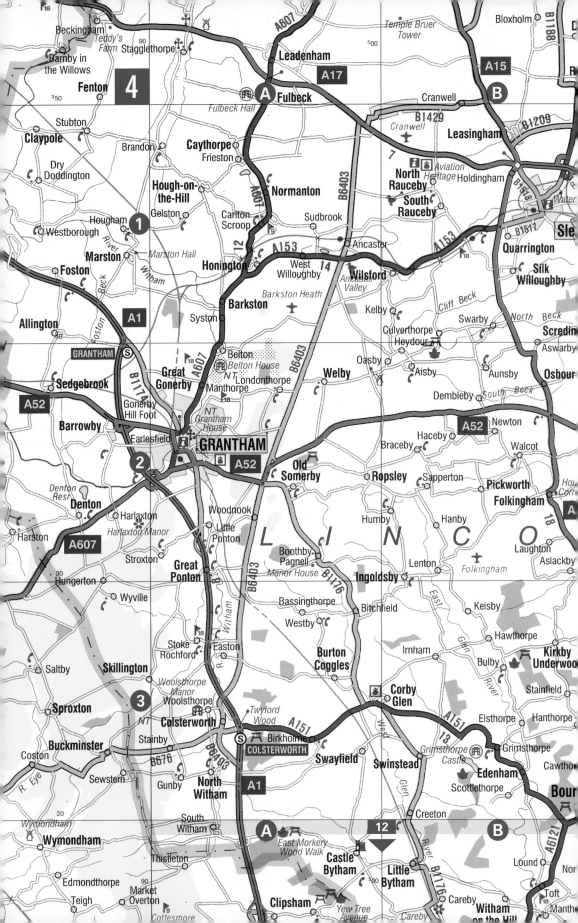

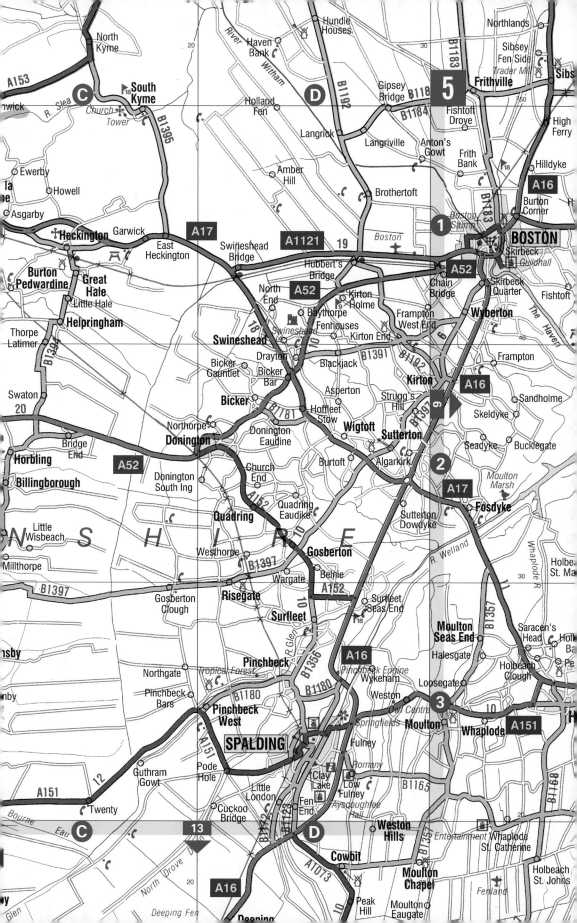

Deeps

60 · 70

Brancaster Bay

Holme Dues
Holme Marsh
Holme Bird
Observatory
Bra
Bra
Titchwell Marsh

Redwell Marsh
1
**Holme next
the Sea**
Titchwell

**Old
Hunstanton**
Hunstanton Cliffs
A149
Thornham

Hunstanton
Sea Life Centre
Ringstead

W A S H
Ringstead Downs

40

*Norfolk
Lavender*
Summerfield

Heacham
∞
B1454
Eaton
Sedgeford
Burntstalk

Snettisham
Southgate
Park Farm
2
Fring

Snettisham Water Mill
Great Bircham

A149
Ingoldisthorpe
Shernborne
**Great
Bircha**

Snettisham
*Shepherd's
Port*

Dersingham
Doddshill
30
Anmer

Dersingham
B1153

*Sandringham
House*
Sandringham

Wolferton
Sandringham
Wolferton Station
**West
Newton**
Water Tower

B1439
Hillington
Flitcham

Babingley
River
Babingley

Terrington Marsh
*Ongar
Hill*
**Castle
Rising**
*Trinity
Hospital*
3

*Castle
Rising*
18
Congham

North Wootton
A148
Grimston

Congham
Hall Herb
Massi

South Wootton
Roydon
Roydon
Common
*Pott
Row*

NORFOLK
A1078
A149
B1153

**Terrington
St. Clement**
Clenchwarton
Gaywood
Ruin
Gayton

Bellmount
A1076
Bawsey

Walpole Wellbank's
ross Keys Orchid World
Fairstead
B1145
Ashwicken
20

*Gayton
Thorpe*

C · A17 · **West Lynn** · 15 · D
Caithness Crystal
Leziate

*Hay
Green*
*Shepherds
Gate*
A47
*Tilney
All Saints*
*Fair
Green*
*Tower
End*
*East
Winch*

*Tilney
High End*
R. Great Ouse
KING'S LYNN
70

*alpole
Peter*
12
Eau Brink
**West
Winch**
Middleton
A47
*East
Walton*

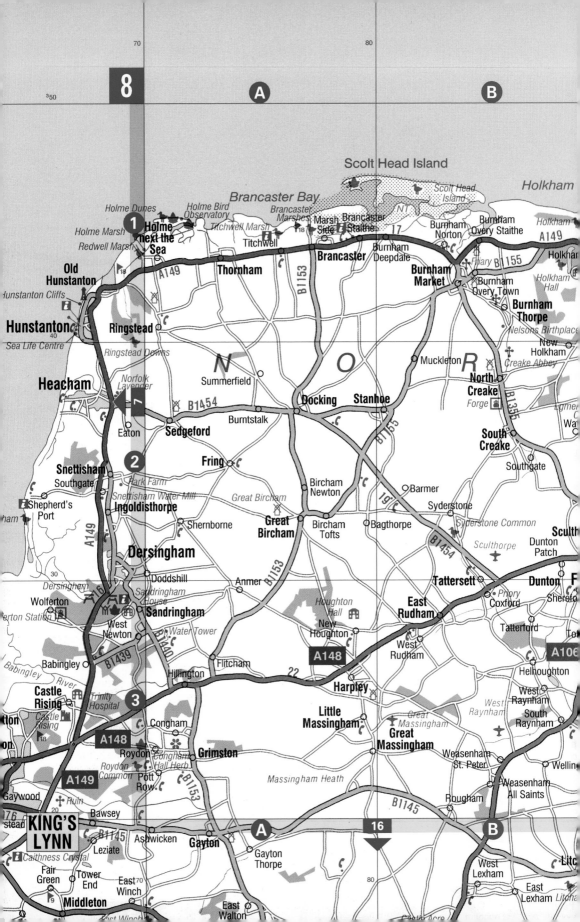

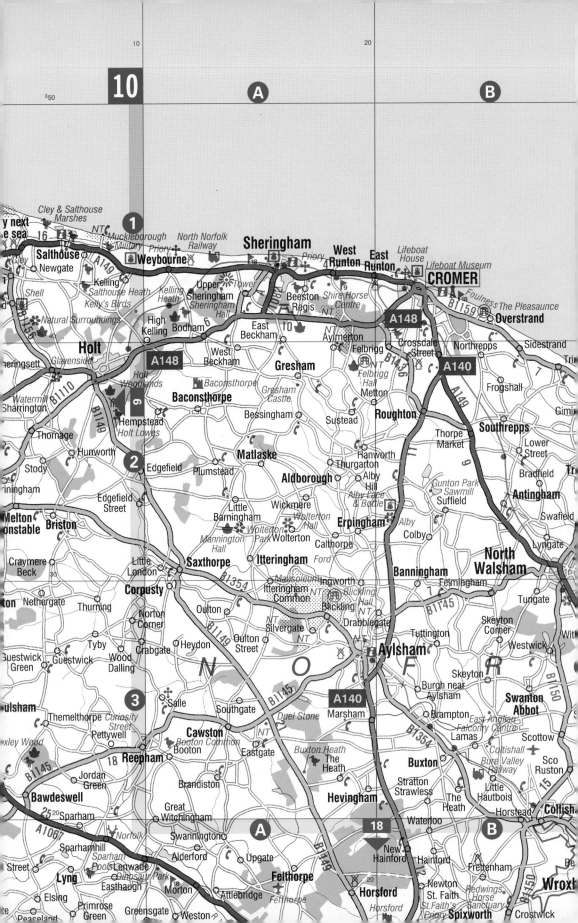

40   ⁶50   ³50

1

40

2

30

3

20

ftonville

Paston
napton
Broomholm
dingthorpe
A150

Bacton
Green
Bacton
Keswick
Priory
Pollard
Street
Walcott
Ostend
Witton
Bridge
Bacton Wood
Ridlington
B1159
11
Happisburgh
Happisburgh
Whimpwell
Green
Eccles on Sea
Hempstead

Horse
mon
Crostwight
Happisburgh
Common
Honing
East
Ruston
Lessingham
Ingham
Corner
Sea Palling
Briggate
Ingham
B1151
Calthorpe
Street
Waxham
L
K
Dilham
Stalham
4
B1159
A149
Stalham
Green
Sutton
Broads
Hickling
Pennygate
Sutton
Hickling
Heath
Hickling
Green
Horsey
NT
Beeston
Hall
Barton
Turf
Water
Trail
Hickling Broad
Horsey
NT
Neatishead
Barton Broad
Catfield
Hickling
Broad
Horsey
Mere
Winterton Dunes
Alderfen
Broad
Irstead
Sharp
Street
How Hill
Catfield
Common
A1151
Dried Flower
Centre
Cangate
C
Haylack
How Hill
Ludham
How Hill
Ludham
19
West
Somerton
East
Somerton
**Winterton-
on-Sea**
Upper
Street
Toad
Hole Cott
Upper
Street
Damgate
D
Martham
Broad
12
Hemsby Hole
oveton
A1062
Johnson's
Street
Cess
Martham
Newport
Horning
Bastwick
Hemsby
Repps
R. Bure
Cockshoot
Broad Broadland
St Benet's
Abbey
Thurne
Rollesby
B1152
B
Ormesby
Scratby

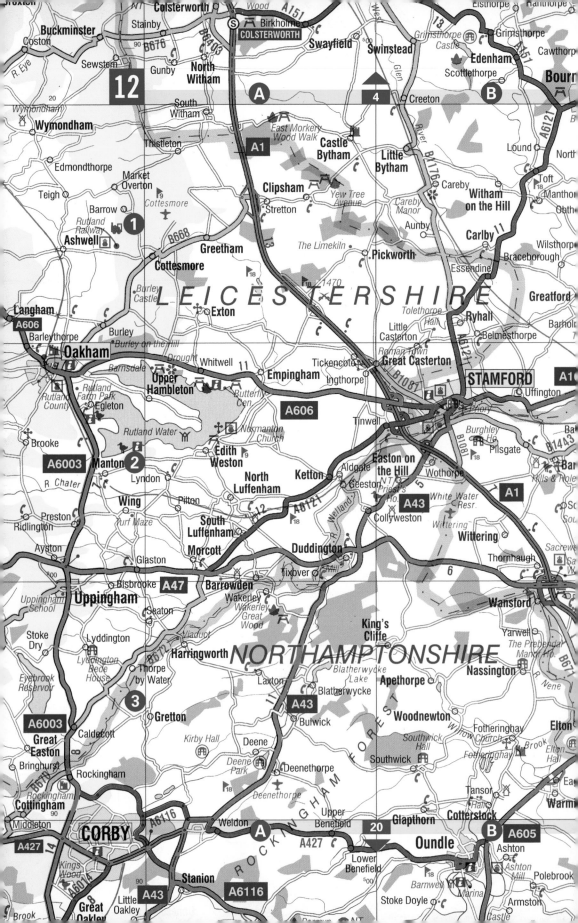

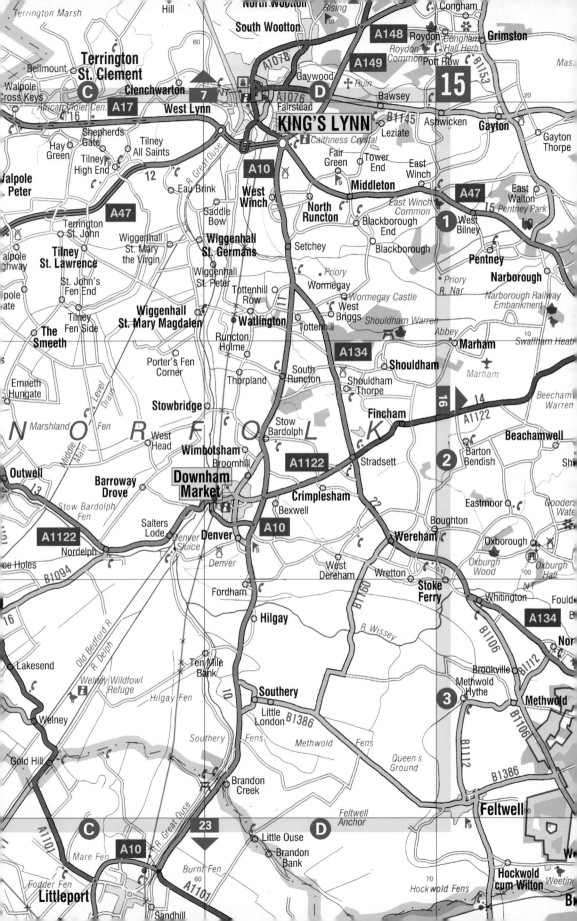

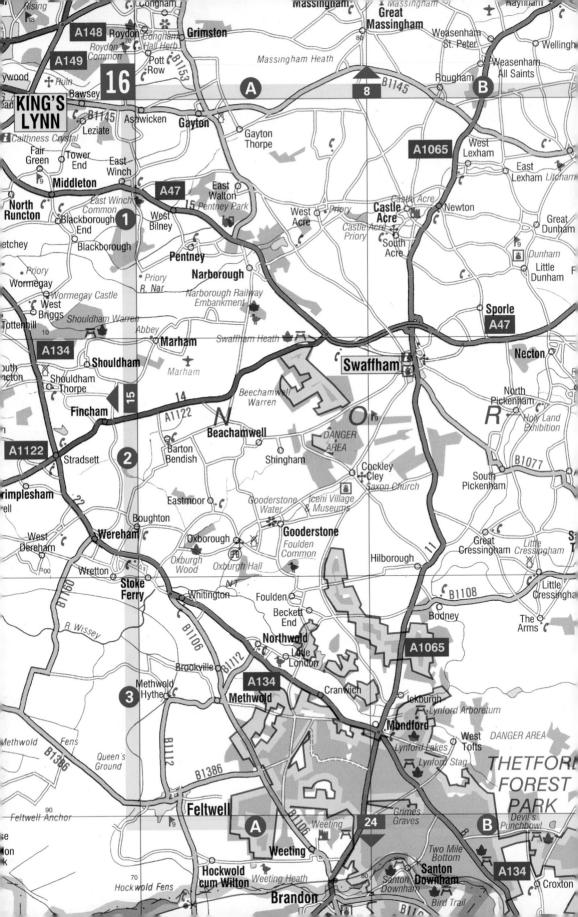

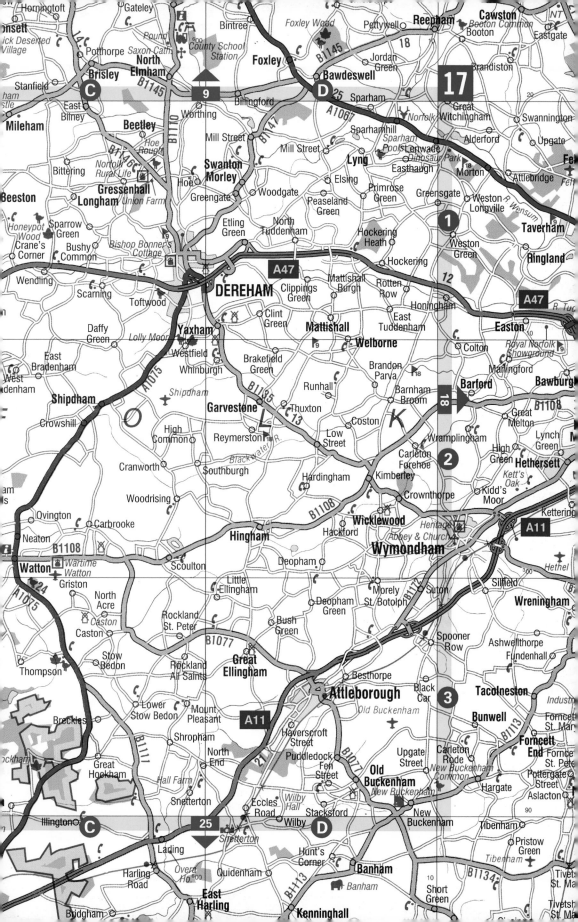

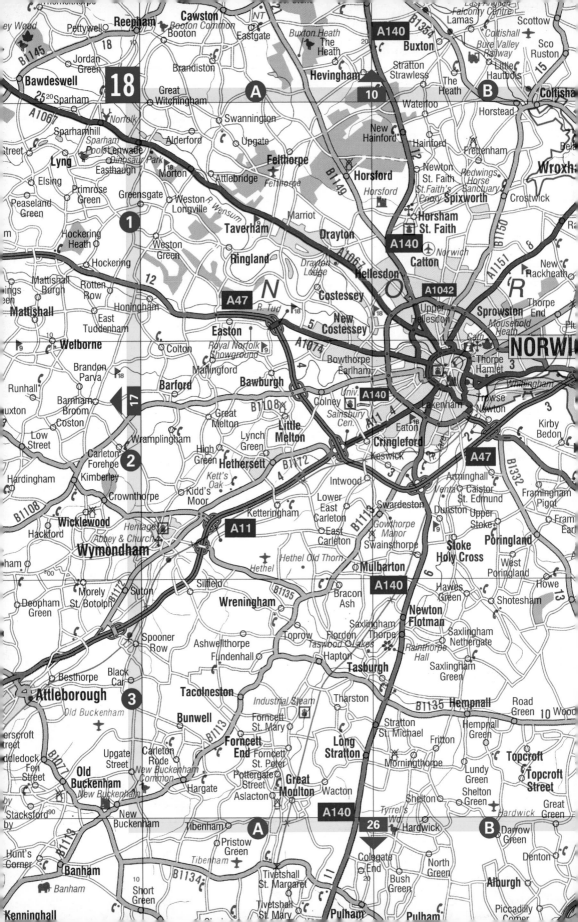

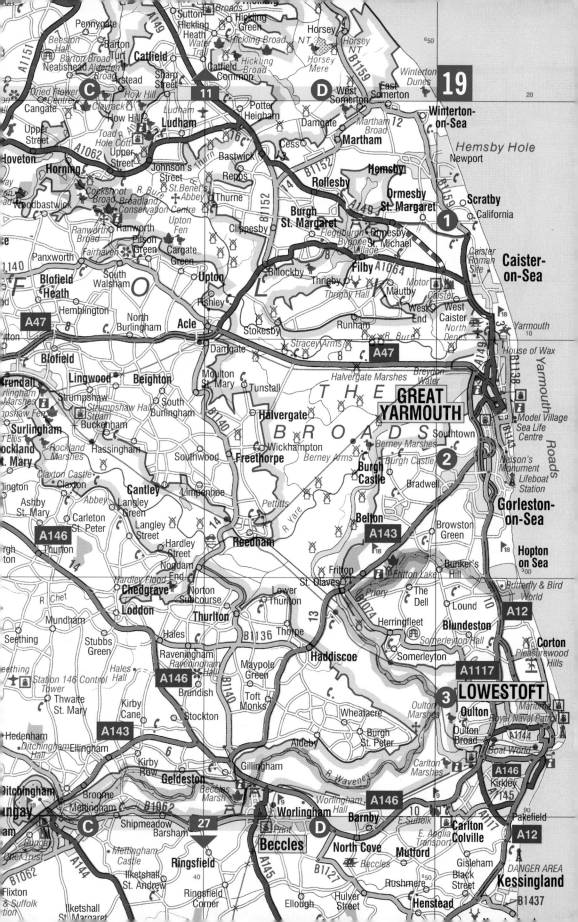

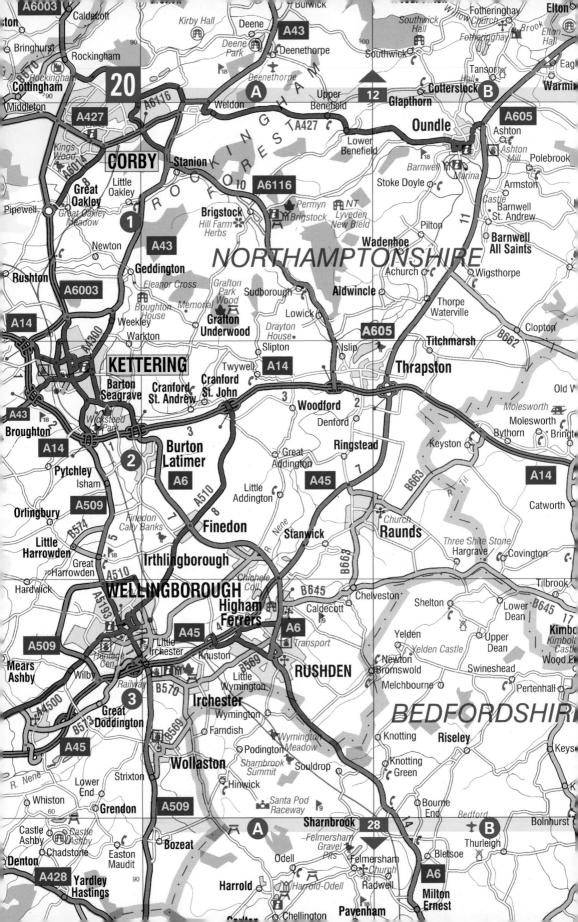

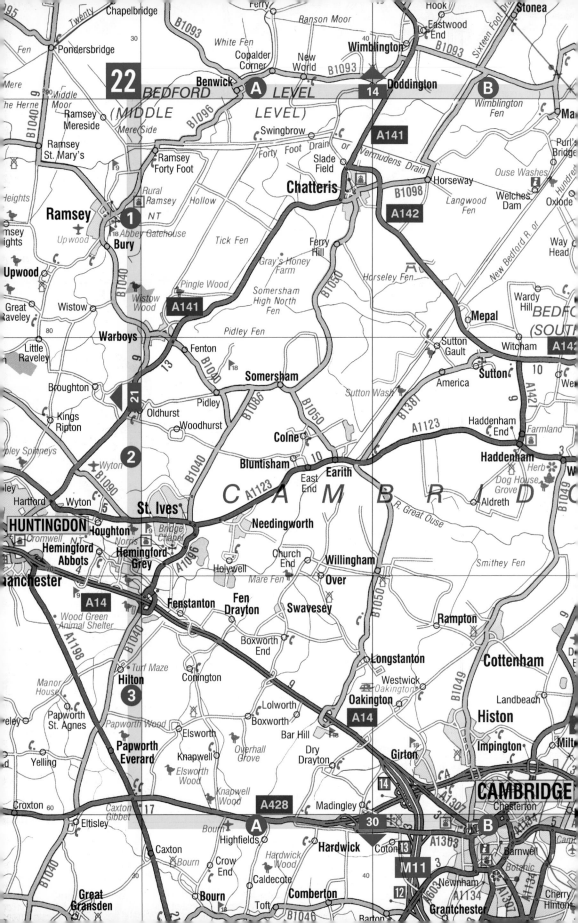

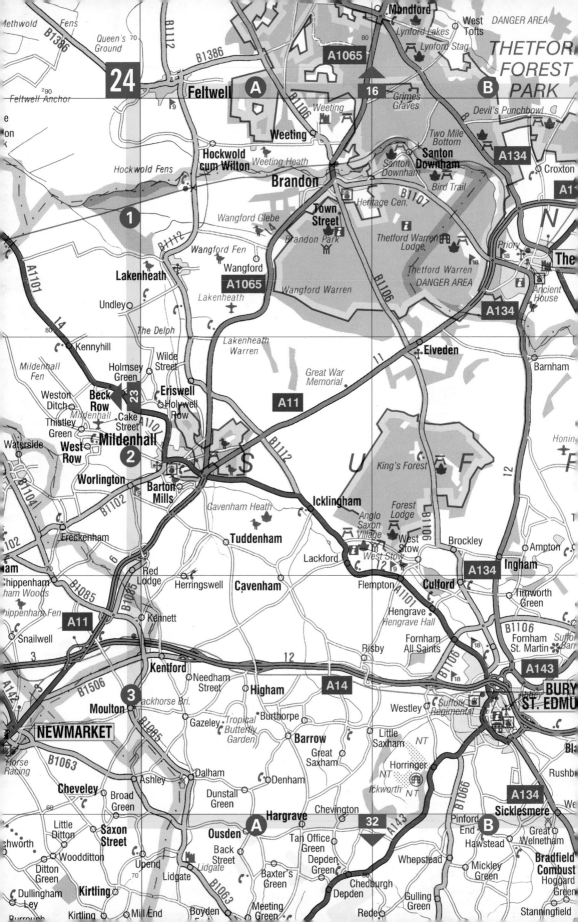

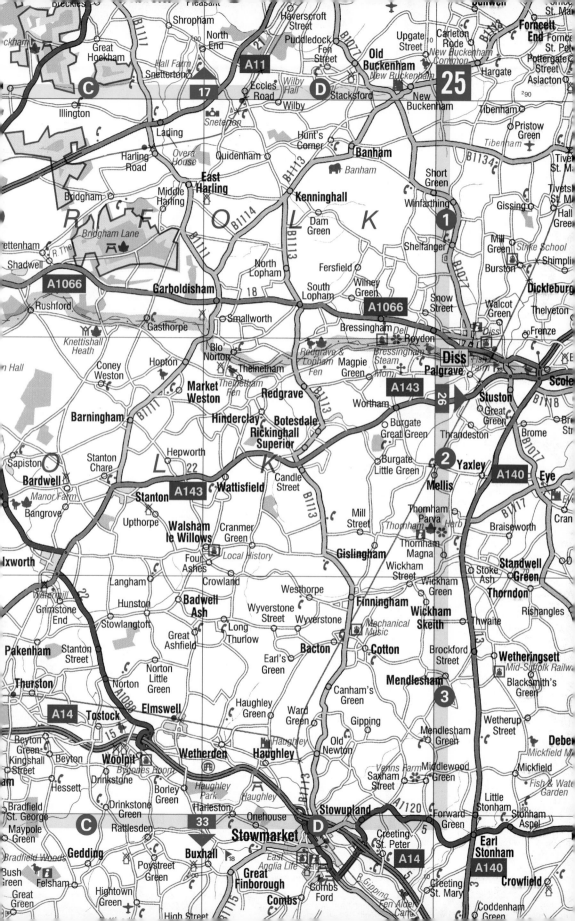

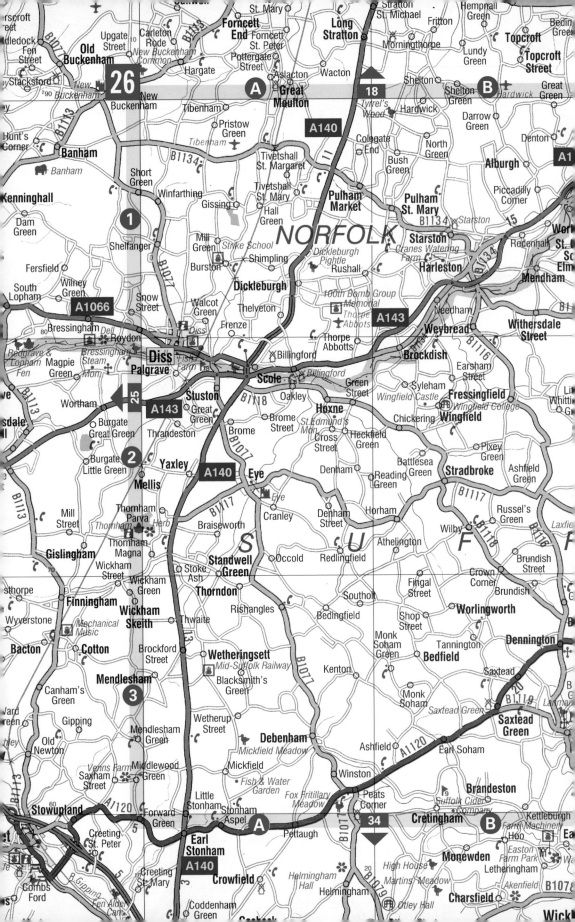

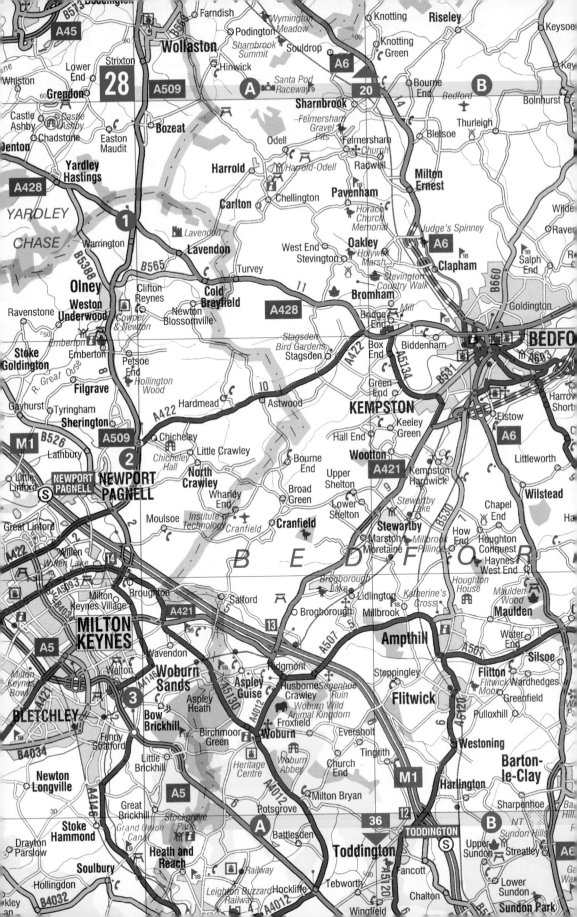

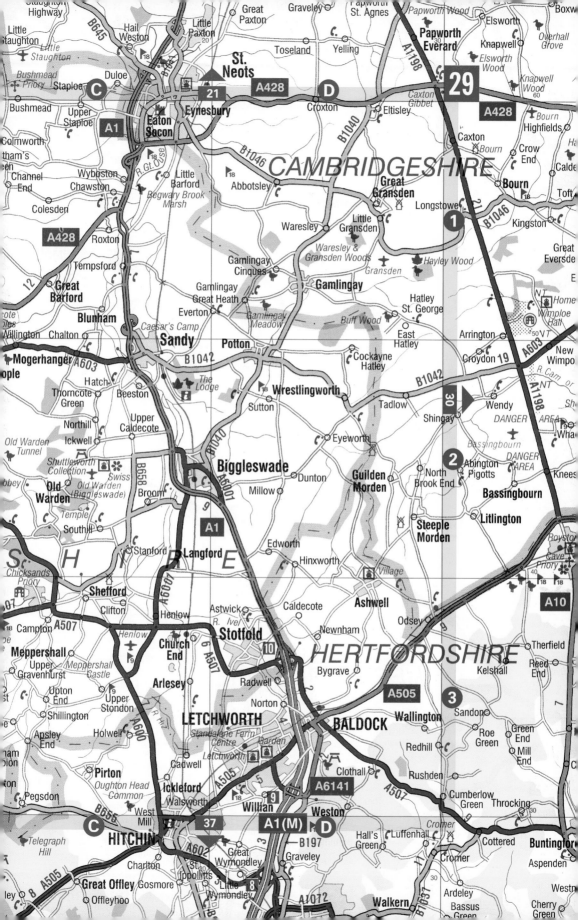

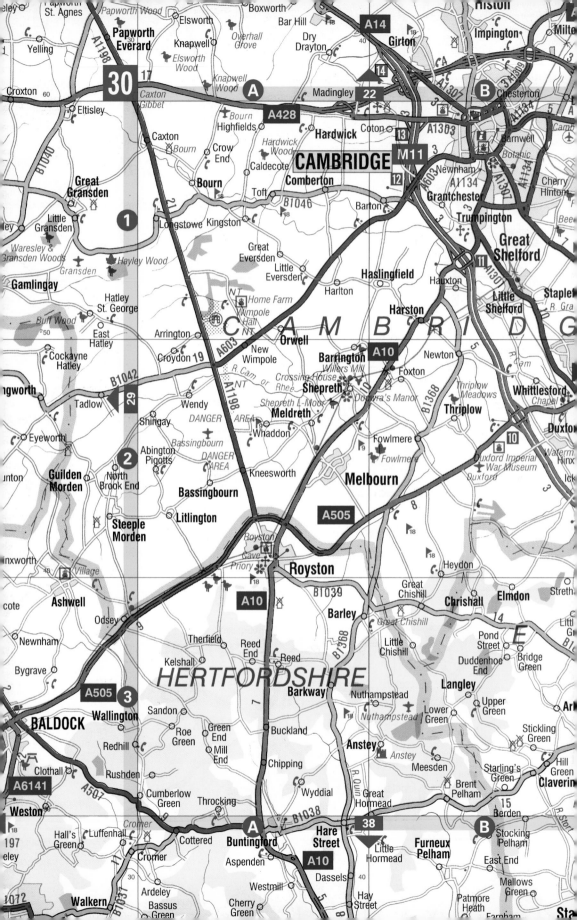

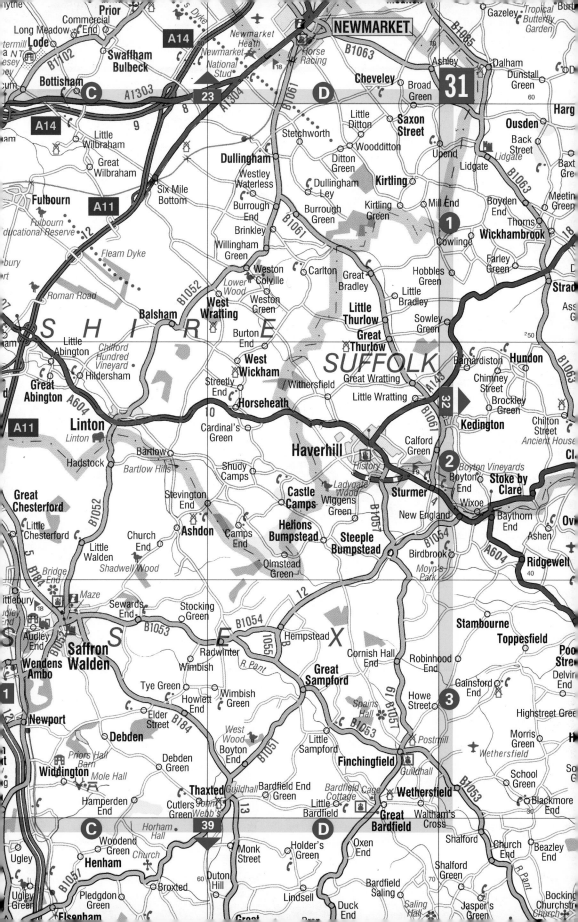

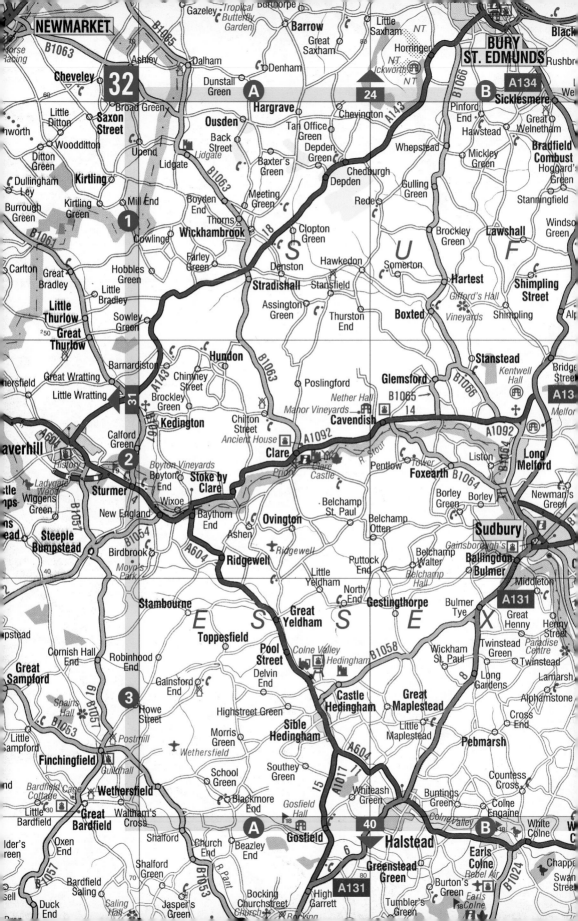

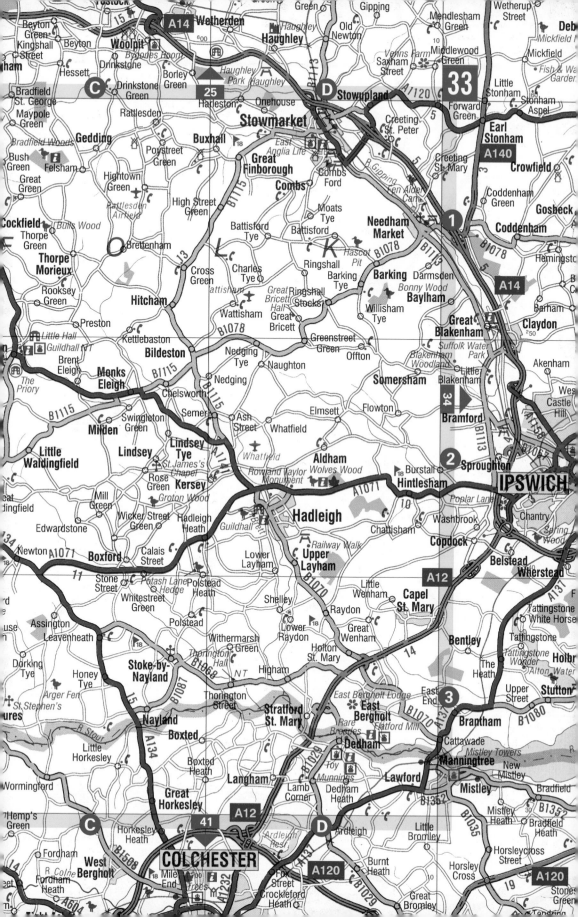

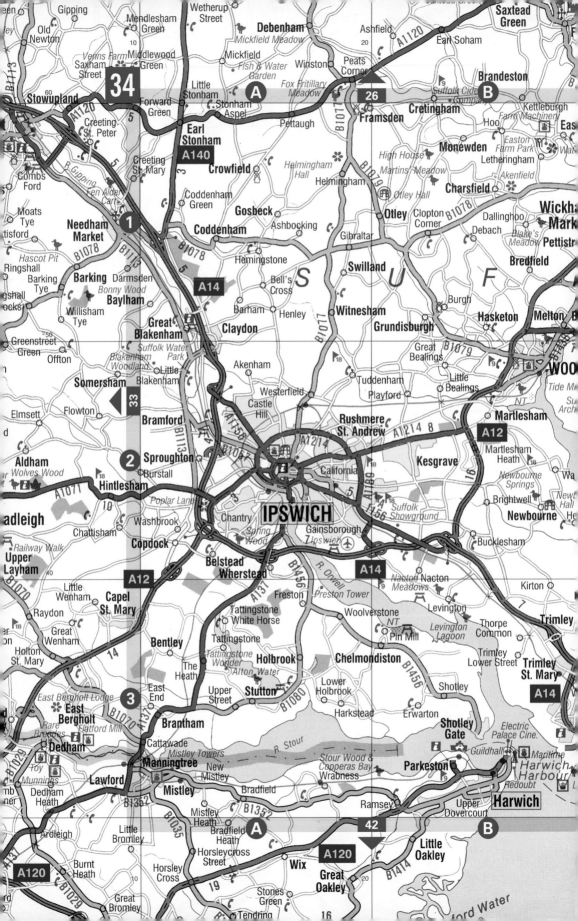

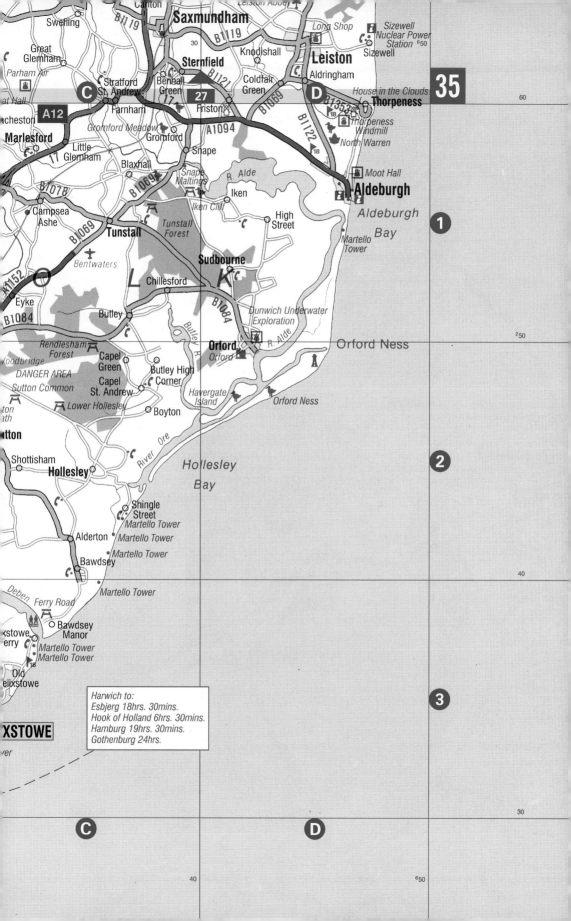

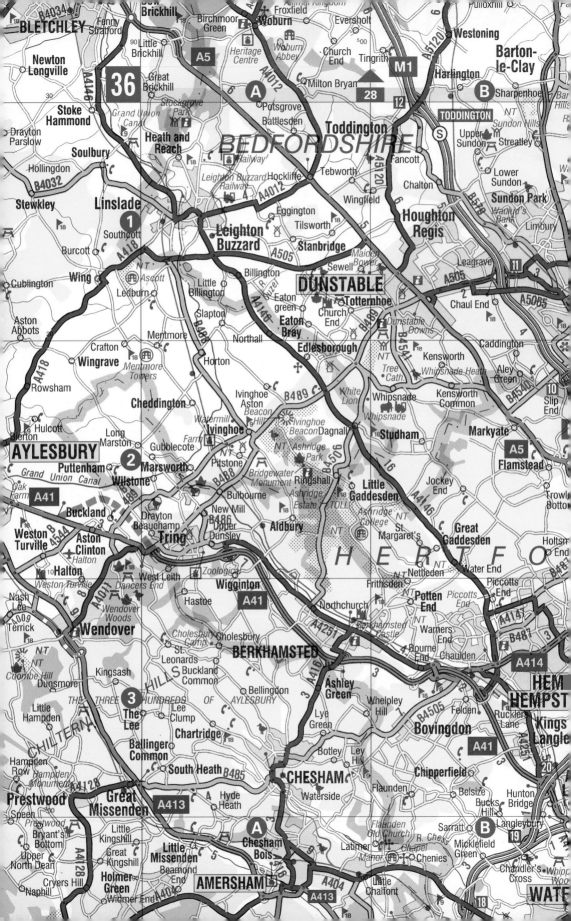

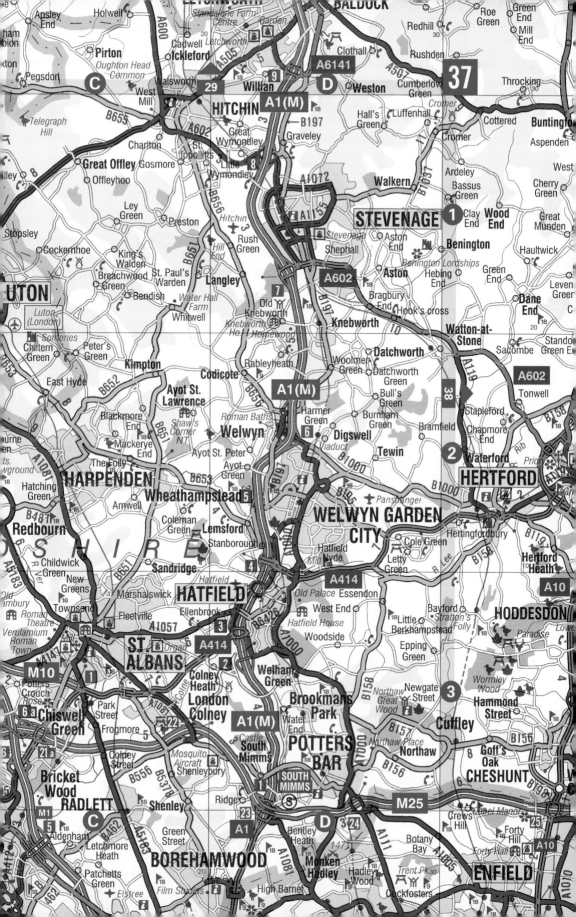

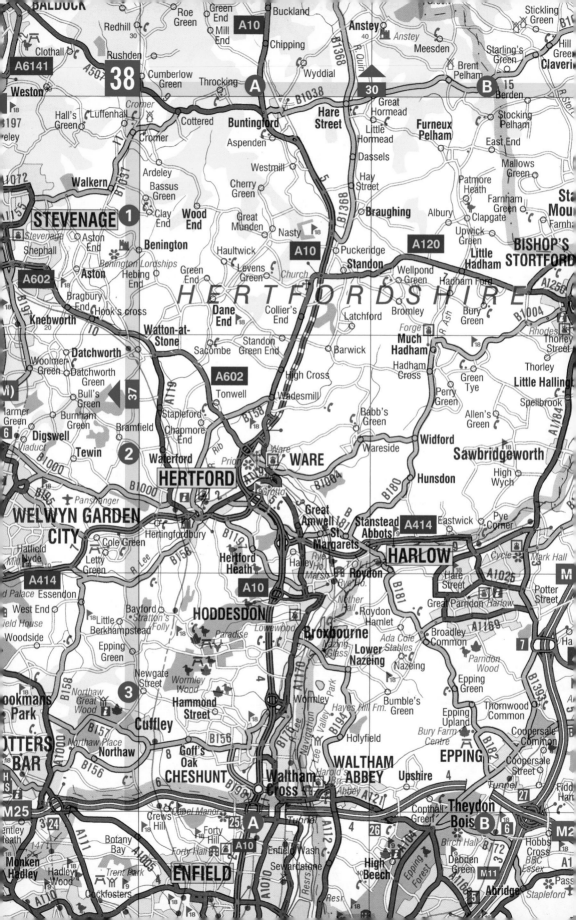

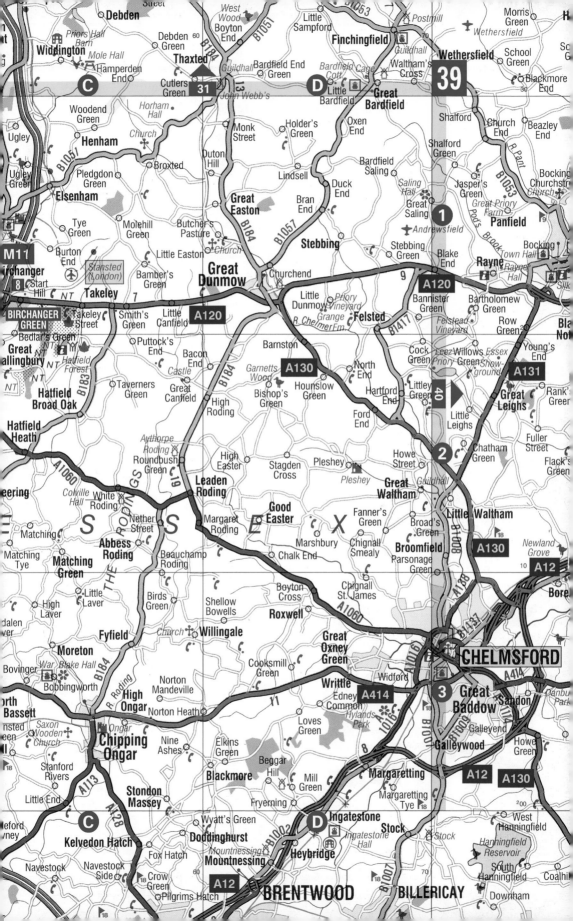

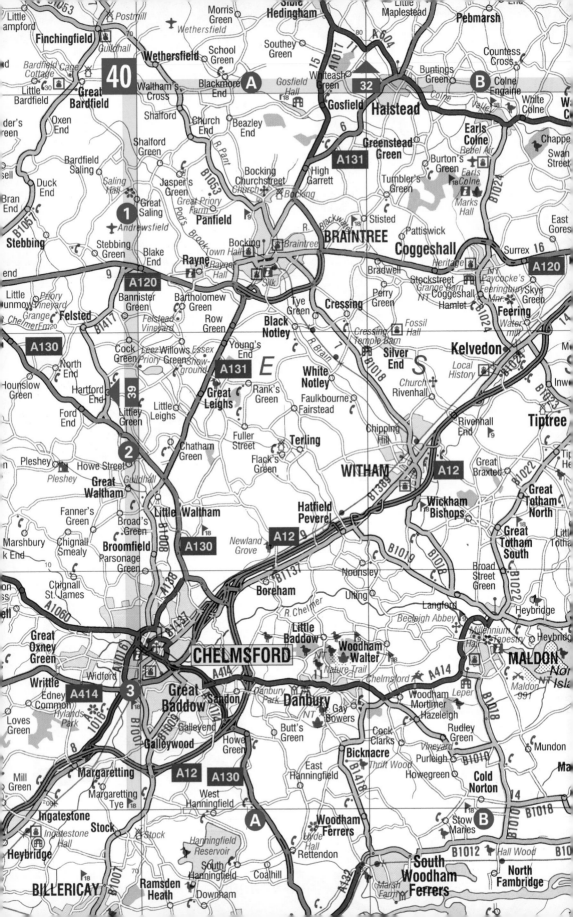

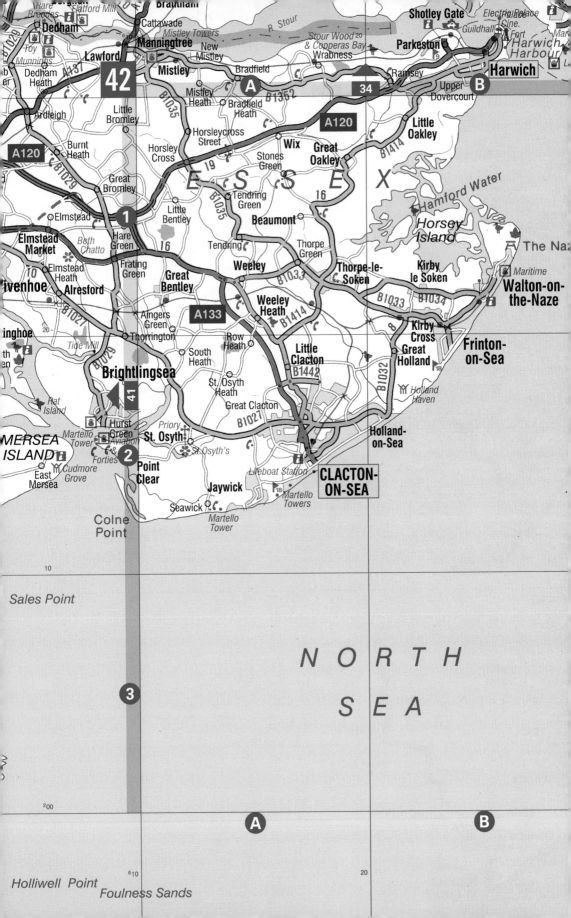

1) A strict alphabetical order is used e.g. Abbotsley follows Abbots Langley but precedes Abbots Ripton.

2) The map reference given refers to the actual map square in which the town spot or built-up area is located and not to the place name.

3) Where two or more places of the same name occur in the same County or Unitary Authority, the nearest large town is also given;
   e.g. Billingford. *Norf* —2A **26** (nr. Diss) indicates that Billingford is located in square 2A on page **26** and is situated near Diss in the County of Norfolk.

COUNTIES AND UNITARY AUTHORITIES with the abbreviations used in this index.

edfordshire : *Beds*	Essex : *Essx*	Leicestershire : *Leic*	Norfolk : *Norf*	Nottinghamshire : *Nott*
uckinghamshire : *Buck*	Greater London : *G.Ln*	Lincolnshire : *Linc*	Northamptonshire : *Nptn*	Suffolk : *Suff*
ambridgeshire : *Camb*	Hertfordshire : *Hert*			

Black Car. *Norf* —3D **17**
Blackheath. *Essx* —1D **41**
Blackheath. *Suff* —2D **27**
Blackjack. *Linc* —2D **5**
Blackmore. *Essx* —3D **39**
Blackmore End. *Essx* —3A **32**
Blackmore End. *Hert* —2C **37**
Black Notley. *Essx* —1A **40**
Blacksmith's Green. *Suff*
—3A **26**
Black Street. *Suff* —1D **27**
Blackthorpe. *Suff* —3C **25**
Blake End. *Essx* —1A **40**
Blakeney. *Norf* —1D **9**
Blatherwycke. *Nptn* —3A **12**
Blaxhall. *Suff* —1C **35**
Bletchley. *Buck* —3A **28**
Bletsoe. *Beds* —1B **28**
Blickling. *Norf* —3A **10**
Blofield. *Norf* —2C **19**
Blofield Heath. *Norf* —1C **19**
Blo' Norton. *Norf* —2D **25**
Bloxholm. *Linc* —1B **4**
Blue Row. *Essx* —2D **41**
Blundeston. *Suff* —3D **19**
Blunham. *Beds* —1C **29**
Bluntisham. *Camb* —2A **22**
Blyford. *Suff* —2D **27**
Blythburgh. *Suff* —2D **27**
Bobbingworth. *Essx* —3C **39**
Bocking. *Essx* —1A **40**
Bocking Churchstreet. *Essx*
—1A **40**
Bodham. *Norf* —1A **10**
Bodney. *Norf* —3B **16**
Bolnhurst. *Beds* —1B **28**
Boothby Pagnell. *Linc* —2A **4**
Booton. *Norf* —3A **10**
Boreham. *Essx* —3A **40**
Borehamwood. *Hert* —3C **37**
Borley. *Essx* —2B **32**
Borley Green. *Essx* —2B **32**
Borley Green. *Suff* —3C **25**
Boston. *Linc* —1A **6**
Botany Bay. *G.Ln* —3D **37**
Botesdale. *Suff* —2D **25**
Botley. *Buck* —3A **36**
Bottisham. *Camb* —3C **23**
Boughton. *Norf* —2D **15**
Bourn. *Camb* —1A **30**
Bourne. *Linc* —3B **4**
Bourne End. *Beds* —2A **28**
(nr. Cranfield)
Bourne End. *Beds* —3B **20**
(nr. Sharnbrook)
Bourne End. *Hert* —3B **36**
Bovingdon. *Hert* —3B **36**
Bovinger. *Essx* —3C **39**
Bow Brickhill. *Buck* —3A **28**
Bowthorpe. *Norf* —2A **18**
Box End. *Beds* —2B **28**
Boxford. *Suff* —2C **33**
Boxted. *Essx* —3C **33**
Boxted. *Suff* —1B **32**
Boxted Heath. *Essx* —3C **33**
Boxworth. *Camb* —3A **22**
Boxworth End. *Camb* —3A **22**
Boyden End. *Suff* —1A **32**
Boyton. *Suff* —2C **35**
Boyton Cross. *Essx* —3D **39**
Boyton End. *Essx* —3D **31**
Boyton End. *Suff* —2A **32**
Bozeat. *Nptn* —1A **28**
Brabling Green. *Suff* —3B **26**
Braceborough. *Linc* —1B **12**
Braceby. *Linc* —2B **4**
Bracon Ash. *Norf* —3A **18**

Bradfield. *Essx* —3A **34**
Bradfield. *Norf* —2B **10**
Bradfield Combust. *Suff*
—1B **32**
Bradfield Heath. *Essx* —1A **42**
Bradfield St Clare. *Suff*
—1C **33**
Bradfield St George. *Suff*
—3C **25**
Bradwell. *Essx* —1B **40**
Bradwell. *Norf* —2D **19**
Bradwell-on-Sea. *Essx*
—3D **41**
Bradwell Waterside. *Essx*
—3C **41**
Bragbury End. *Hert* —1D **37**
Braintree. *Essx* —1A **40**
Braiseworth. *Suff* —2A **26**
Brakefield Green. *Norf*
—2D **17**
Bramerton. *Norf* —2B **18**
Bramfield. *Hert* —2D **37**
Bramfield. *Suff* —2C **27**
Bramford. *Suff* —2A **34**
Brampton. *Camb* —2D **21**
Brampton. *Norf* —3B **10**
Brampton. *Suff* —1D **27**
Brancaster. *Norf* —1A **8**
Brancaster Staith. *Norf*
—1A **8**
Brand End. *Linc* —1A **6**
Brandeston. *Suff* —3B **26**
Brandiston. *Norf* —3A **10**
Brandon. *Linc* —1A **4**
Brandon. *Suff* —1A **24**
Brandon Bank. *Camb* —1D **23**
Brandon Creek. *Norf* —3D **15**
Brandon Parva. *Norf* —2D **17**
Bran End. *Essx* —1D **39**
Brantham. *Suff* —3A **34**
Braughing. *Hert* —1A **38**
Breachwood Green. *Hert*
—1C **37**
Breckles. *Norf* —3C **17**
Bredfield. *Suff* —1B **34**
Brent Eleigh. *Suff* —2C **33**
Brent Pelham. *Hert* —3B **30**
Bressingham. *Norf* —1D **25**
Brettenham. *Norf* —1C **25**
Brettenham. *Suff* —1C **33**
Bricket Wood. *Hert* —3C **37**
Bridge End. *Beds* —1B **28**
Bridge End. *Linc* —2C **5**
Bridge Green. *Essx* —3B **30**
Bridge Street. *Suff* —2B **32**
Bridgham. *Norf* —1C **25**
Briggate. *Norf* —3C **11**
Brightlingsea. *Essx* —2D **41**
Brightwell. *Suff* —2B **34**
Brigstock. *Nptn* —1A **20**
Bringhurst. *Leic* —3A **12**
Brington. *Camb* —2B **20**
Briningham. *Norf* —2D **9**
Brinkley. *Camb* —1D **31**
Brinton. *Norf* —2D **9**
Brisley. *Norf* —3C **9**
Briston. *Norf* —2D **9**
Broad Green. *Beds* —2A **28**
Broad Green. *Camb* —1D **31**
Broad Hill. *Camb* —2C **23**
Broadley Common. *Essx*
—3B **38**
Broad's Green. *Essx* —2D **39**
Broad Street Green. *Essx*
—3B **40**
Broadway. *Suff* —2C **27**
Brockdish. *Norf* —2B **26**

Brockford Street. *Suff*
—3A **26**
Brockley. *Suff* —2B **24**
Brockley Green. *Suff* —2A **32**
(nr. Bury St Edmunds)
Brockley Green. *Suff* —1B **32**
(nr. Haverhill)
Brogborough. *Beds* —3A **28**
Brome. *Suff* —2A **26**
Brome Street. *Suff* —2A **26**
Bromeswell. *Suff* —1C **35**
Bromham. *Beds* —1B **28**
Bromley. *Hert* —1B **38**
Brooke. *Leic* —2A **12**
Brooke. *Norf* —3B **18**
Brookmans Park. *Hert*
—3D **37**
Brookville. *Norf* —3A **16**
Broom. *Beds* —2C **29**
Broome. *Norf* —3C **19**
Broomfield. *Essx* —2A **40**
Broom Green. *Norf* —3C **9**
Broomhill. *Norf* —2D **15**
Broomholm. *Norf* —2C **11**
Brotherhouse Bar. *Linc*
—1D **13**
Brothertoft. *Linc* —1D **5**
Broughton. *Buck* —3A **28**
Broughton. *Camb* —2D **21**
Browston Green. *Norf*
—2D **19**
Broxbourne. *Hert* —3A **38**
Broxted. *Essx* —1C **39**
Bruisyard. *Suff* —3C **27**
Bruisyard Street. *Suff*
—3C **27**
Brundall. *Norf* —2C **19**
Brundish. *Norf* —3C **19**
Brundish. *Suff* —3B **26**
Brundish Street. *Suff* —2B **26**
Buckden. *Camb* —3C **21**
Buckenham. *Norf* —2C **19**
Buckland. *Buck* —2A **36**
Buckland. *Hert* —3A **30**
Buckland Common. *Buck*
—3A **36**
Bucklegate. *Linc* —2A **6**
Bucklesham. *Suff* —2B **34**
Buckminster. *Leic* —3A **4**
Bucks Hill. *Hert* —3B **36**
Buckworth. *Camb* —2C **21**
Bulbourne. *Hert* —2A **36**
Bulby. *Linc* —3B **4**
Bull's Green. *Hert* —2D **37**
Bulmer. *Essx* —2B **32**
Bulmer Tye. *Essx* —3B **32**
Bulwick. *Nptn* —3A **12**
Bumble's Green. *Essx*
—3B **38**
Bungay. *Suff* —1C **27**
Bunker's Hill. *Camb* —2B **14**
Bunker's Hill. *Suff* —2D **19**
Buntingford. *Hert* —1A **38**
Buntings Green. *Essx* —3B **32**
Bunwell. *Norf* —3A **18**
Burcott. *Buck* —1A **36**
Bures. *Suff* —3C **33**
Burgate Great Green. *Suff*
—2D **25**
Burgate Little Green. *Suff*
—2D **25**
Burgh. *Suff* —1B **34**
Burgh Castle. *Norf* —2D **19**
Burgh near Aylsham. *Norf*
—3B **10**
Burgh St Margaret. *Norf*
—1D **19**

Burgh St Peter. *Norf* —3D **19**
Burley. *Leic* —1A **12**
Burnham Deepdale. *Norf*
—1B **8**
Burnham Green. *Hert* —2D **37**
Burnham Market. *Norf* —1B **8**
Burnham Norton. *Norf* —1B **8**
Burnham-on-Crouch. *Essx*
—3C **41**
Burnham Overy Staithe. *Norf*
—1B **8**
Burnham Overy Town. *Norf*
—1B **8**
Burnham Thorpe. *Norf* —1B **8**
Burnt Heath. *Essx* —1D **41**
Burntstalk. *Norf* —2A **8**
Burrough End. *Camb* —1D **31**
Burrough Green. *Camb*
—1D **31**
Burstall. *Suff* —2D **33**
Burston. *Norf* —1A **26**
Burthorpe. *Suff* —3A **24**
Burtoft. *Linc* —2D **5**
Burton Coggles. *Linc* —3A **4**
Burton Corner. *Linc* —1A **6**
Burton End. *Camb* —2D **31**
Burton End. *Essx* —1C **39**
Burton Latimer. *Nptn* —2A **20**
Burton Pedwardine. *Linc*
—1C **5**
Burton's Green. *Essx* —1B **40**
Burwell. *Camb* —3C **23**
Bury. *Camb* —1D **21**
Bury Green. *Hert* —1B **38**
Bury St Edmunds. *Suff*
—3B **24**
Bush Green. *Norf* —3D **17**
(nr. Attleborough)
Bush Green. *Norf* —1B **26**
(nr. Harleston)
Bush Green. *Suff* —1C **33**
Bushmead. *Beds* —3C **21**
Bushy Common. *Norf*
—1C **17**
Bustard Green. *Essx* —1D **39**
Butcher's Pasture. *Essx*
—1D **39**
Butley. *Suff* —1C **35**
Butley High Corner. *Suff*
—2C **35**
Butterwick. *Linc* —1A **6**
Butt's Green. *Essx* —3A **40**
Buxhall. *Suff* —1D **33**
Buxton. *Norf* —3B **10**
Bygrave. *Hert* —3D **29**
Bythorn. *Camb* —2B **20**

Caddington. *Beds* —2B **36**
Cadwell. *Hert* —3C **29**
Caister-on-Sea. *Norf* —1D **19**
Caister St Edmund. *Norf*
—2B **18**
Cake Street. *Suff* —2D **23**
Calais Street. *Suff* —2C **33**
Caldecote. *Camb* —1A **30**
(nr. Cambridge)
Caldecote. *Camb* —1C **21**
(nr. Peterborough)
Caldecote. *Hert* —3D **29**
Caldecott. *Leic* —3A **12**
Caldecott. *Nptn* —3A **20**
Calford Green. *Suff* —2D **31**
California. *Norf* —1D **19**
California. *Suff* —2A **34**
Calthorpe. *Norf* —2A **10**
Calthorpe Street. *Norf* —3D **11**

Cambridge. *Camb* —1B **30**
Campsea Ashe. *Suff* —1C **35**
Camps End. *Camb* —2D **31**
Campton. *Beds* —3C **29**
Candle Street. *Suff* —2D **25**
Cangate. *Norf* —3C **11**
Canham's Green. *Suff*
—3D **2**
Cantley. *Norf* —2C **19**
Capel Green. *Suff* —2C **35**
Capel St Andrew. *Suff*
—2C **3**
Capel St Mary. *Suff* —3D **3**
Carbrooke. *Norf* —2C **17**
Cardinal's Green. *Camb*
—2D **3**
Cardington. *Beds* —2B **28**
Careby. *Linc* —1B **12**
Cargate Green. *Norf* —1C **19**
Carlby. *Linc* —1B **12**
Carleton Forehoe. *Norf*
—2D **1**
Carleton Rode. *Norf* —3A **18**
Carleton St Peter. *Norf*
—2C **1**
Carlton. *Beds* —1A **28**
Carlton. *Camb* —1D **31**
Carlton. *Suff* —3C **27**
Carlton Colville. *Suff* —3D **1**
Carlton Scroop. *Linc* —1A **4**
Castle Acre. *Norf* —1B **16**
Castle Ashby. *Nptn* —1A **28**
Castle Bytham. *Linc* —1A **12**
Castle Camps. *Camb* —2D **3**
Castle Hedingham. *Essx*
—3A **3**
Castle Hill. *Suff* —2A **34**
Castle Rising. *Norf* —3D **7**
Caston. *Norf* —3C **17**
Castor. *Camb* —3C **13**
Catfield. *Norf* —3C **11**
Catfield Common. *Norf*
—3C **1**
Cattawade. *Suff* —3A **34**
Catton. *Norf* —1B **18**
Catworth. *Camb* —2B **20**
Cavendish. *Suff* —2B **32**
Cavenham. *Suff* —3A **24**
Cawston. *Norf* —3A **10**
Cawthorpe. *Linc* —3B **4**
Caxton. *Camb* —1A **30**
Caythorpe. *Linc* —1A **4**
Cess. *Norf* —1D **19**
Chadstone. *Nptn* —1A **28**
Chainbridge. *Camb* —2B **14**
Chain Bridge. *Linc* —1A **6**
Chalk End. *Essx* —2D **39**
Chalton. *Beds* —1C **29**
(nr. Bedford)
Chalton. *Beds* —1B **36**
(nr. Luton)
Chandler's Cross. *Hert*
—3B **3**
Channel End. *Beds* —1C **29**
Chantry. *Suff* —2A **34**
Chapelbridge. *Camb* —3D **13**
Chapel End. *Beds* —2B **28**
Chapelgate. *Linc* —3B **6**
Chapmore End. *Hert* —2A **38**
Chappel. *Essx* —1B **40**
Charles Tye. *Suff* —1D **33**
Charlton. *Hert* —1C **37**
Charsfield. *Suff* —1B **34**
Chartridge. *Buck* —3A **36**
Chatham Green. *Essx* —2A **4**
Chatteris. *Camb* —1A **22**
Chattisham. *Suff* —2D **33**

Earlesfield. *Linc* —2A **4**
Earlham. *Norf* —2A **18**
Earls Colne. *Essx* —1B **40**
Earl's Green. *Suff* —3D **25**
Earl Soham. *Suff* —3B **26**
Earl Stonham. *Suff* —1A **34**
Earsham. *Norf* —1C **27**
Earsham Street. *Suff* —2B **26**
East Barsham. *Norf* —2C **9**
East Beckham. *Norf* —1A **10**
East Bergholt. *Suff* —3D **33**
East Bliney. *Norf* —1C **17**
East Bradenham. *Norf*
　—2C **17**
East Bridge. *Suff* —3D **27**
East Carleton. *Norf* —2A **18**
East End. *Camb* —2A **22**
East End. *Hert* —1B **38**
East End. *Suff* —3A **34**
Eastgate. *Norf* —3A **10**
East Gores. *Essx* —1B **40**
East Hanningfield. *Essx*
　—3A **40**
East Harling. *Norf* —1C **25**
East Hatley. *Camb* —1D **29**
Easthaugh. *Norf* —1D **17**
East Heckington. *Linc* —1C **5**
Easthorpe. *Essx* —1C **41**
East Hyde. *Beds* —2C **37**
East Lexham. *Norf* —1B **16**
East Mersea. *Essx* —2D **41**
Eastmoor. *Norf* —2A **16**
Easton. *Camb* —2C **21**
Easton. *Linc* —3A **4**
Easton. *Norf* —1A **18**
Easton. *Suff* —1B **34**
Easton Maudit. *Nptn* —1A **28**
Easton on the Hill. *Nptn*
　—2B **12**
East Perry. *Camb* —3C **21**
East Raynham. *Norf* —3B **8**
Eastrea. *Camb* —3D **13**
East Rudham. *Norf* —3B **8**
East Runton. *Norf* —1A **10**
East Ruston. *Norf* —3C **11**
East Somerton. *Norf* —1D **19**
East Tuddenham. *Norf*
　—1D **17**
East Walton. *Norf* —1A **16**
Eastwick. *Hert* —2B **38**
East Winch. *Norf* —1D **15**
Eastwood End. *Camb* —3B **14**
Eaton. *Norf* —2D **7**
　(nr. Heacham)
Eaton. *Norf* —2B **18**
　(nr. Norwich)
Eaton Bray. *Beds* —1A **36**
Eaton Green. *Beds* —1A **36**
Eaton Socon. *Camb* —1C **29**
Eau Brink. *Norf* —1C **15**
Eccles on Sea. *Norf* —3D **11**
Eccles Road. *Norf* —3D **17**
Edenham. *Linc* —3B **4**
Edgefield. *Norf* —2D **9**
Edgefield Street. *Norf* —2D **9**
Edingthorpe. *Norf* —2C **11**
Edith Weston. *Leic* —2A **12**
Edlesborough. *Buck* —2A **36**
Edmondthorpe. *Leic* —1A **12**
Edney Common. *Essx*
　—3D **39**
Edwardstone. *Suff* —2C **33**
Edworth. *Beds* —2D **29**
Eggington. *Beds* —1A **36**
Egleton. *Leic* —2A **12**
Eight Ash Green. *Essx*
　—1C **41**

Eldernell. *Camb* —3A **14**
Elder Street. *Essx* —3C **31**
Elford Closes. *Camb* —2B **22**
Elkins Green. *Essx* —3D **39**
Ellenbrook. *Hert* —3D **37**
Ellingham. *Norf* —3C **19**
Ellington. *Camb* —2C **21**
Ellington Thorpe. *Camb*
　—2C **21**
Ellough. *Suff* —1D **27**
Elm. *Camb* —2B **14**
Elmdon. *Essx* —3B **30**
Elmsett. *Suff* —2D **33**
Elmstead. *Essx* —1D **41**
Elmstead Heath. *Essx*
　—1D **41**
Elmstead Market. *Essx*
　—1D **41**
Elmswell. *Suff* —3C **25**
Elsenham. *Essx* —1C **39**
Elsing. *Norf* —1D **17**
Elsthorpe. *Linc* —3B **4**
Elstow. *Beds* —2B **28**
Elsworth. *Camb* —3A **22**
Eltisley. *Camb* —1D **29**
Elton. *Camb* —3B **12**
Elveden. *Suff* —2B **24**
Ely. *Camb* —1C **23**
Emberton. *Buck* —2A **28**
Emneth. *Norf* —2B **14**
Emneth Hungate. *Norf*
　—2C **15**
Empingham. *Leic* —2A **12**
Enfield. *G.Ln* —3A **38**
Enfield Wash. *G.Ln* —3A **38**
Epping. *Essx* —3B **38**
Epping Green. *Essx* —3B **38**
Epping Green. *Hert* —3D **37**
Epping Upland. *Essx* —3B **38**
Eriswell. *Suff* —2A **24**
Erpingham. *Norf* —2A **10**
Erwarton. *Suff* —3B **34**
Essendine. *Leic* —1B **12**
Essendon. *Hert* —3D **37**
Etling Green. *Norf* —1D **17**
Etton. *Camb* —2C **13**
Euston. *Suff* —2B **24**
Evedon. *Linc* —1B **4**
Eversholt. *Beds* —3A **28**
Everton. *Beds* —1D **29**
Ewerby. *Linc* —1C **5**
Exning. *Suff* —3D **23**
Exton. *Leic* —1A **12**
Eye. *Camb* —2D **13**
Eye. *Suff* —2A **26**
Eye Green. *Camb* —2D **13**
Eyeworth. *Beds* —2D **29**
Eyke. *Suff* —1C **35**
Eynesbury. *Camb* —1C **29**

Fair Green. *Norf* —1D **15**
Fairstead. *Essx* —2A **40**
Fairstead. *Norf* —1D **15**
Fakenham. *Norf* —3C **9**
Falkenham. *Suff* —3B **34**
Fancott. *Beds* —1B **36**
Fanner's Green. *Essx* —2D **39**
Farley Green. *Suff* —1A **32**
Farndish. *Beds* —3A **20**
Farnham. *Essx* —1B **38**
Farnham. *Suff* —3C **27**
Farnham Green. *Essx* —1B **38**
Faulkbourne. *Essx* —2A **40**
Feering. *Essx* —1B **40**
Felbrigg. *Norf* —2B **10**
Felden. *Hert* —3B **36**

Felixstowe. *Suff* —3B **34**
Felixstowe Ferry. *Suff* —3C **35**
Felmersham. *Beds* —1A **28**
Felmingham. *Norf* —3B **10**
Felsham. *Suff* —1C **33**
Felsted. *Essx* —1D **39**
Felthorpe. *Norf* —1A **18**
Feltwell. *Norf* —3A **16**
Fen Ditton. *Camb* —3B **22**
Fen Drayton. *Camb* —3A **22**
Fen End. *Linc* —3D **5**
Fenhouses. *Linc* —1D **5**
Fenny Stratford. *Buck*
　—3A **28**
Fenstanton. *Camb* —3A **22**
Fen Street. *Norf* —3D **17**
Fenton. *Camb* —2A **22**
Ferry Hill. *Camb* —1A **22**
Fersfield. *Norf* —1D **25**
Fiddlers Hamlet. *Essx* —3B **38**
Field Dalling. *Norf* —2D **9**
Filby. *Norf* —1D **19**
Filgrave. *Buck* —2A **28**
Fincham. *Norf* —2D **15**
Finchingfield. *Essx* —3D **31**
Finedon. *Nptn* —2A **20**
Fingal Street. *Suff* —2B **26**
Fingringhoe. *Essx* —1D **41**
Finningham. *Suff* —3D **25**
Fishley. *Norf* —1D **19**
Fishtoft. *Linc* —1A **6**
Fishtoft Drove. *Linc* —1A **6**
Fitton End. *Camb* —1B **14**
Flack's Green. *Essx* —2A **40**
Flamstead. *Hert* —2B **36**
Flaunden. *Hert* —3B **36**
Fleet. *Linc* —3A **6**
Fleet Hargate. *Linc* —3A **6**
Fleetville. *Hert* —3C **37**
Flempton. *Suff* —3B **24**
Flitcham. *Norf* —3A **8**
Flitton. *Beds* —3B **28**
Flitwick. *Beds* —3B **28**
Flixton. *Suff* —1C **27**
Flood's Ferry. *Camb* —3A **14**
Flordon. *Norf* —3A **18**
Flowton. *Suff* —2D **33**
Folkingham. *Linc* —2B **4**
Folksworth. *Camb* —3C **13**
Folly, The. *Hert* —2C **37**
Ford End. *Essx* —2D **39**
Fordham. *Camb* —2D **23**
Fordham. *Essx* —1C **41**
Fordham. *Norf* —3D **15**
Fordham Heath. *Essx* —1C **41**
Fordstreet. *Essx* —1C **41**
Forncett End. *Norf* —3A **18**
Forncett St Mary. *Norf*
　—3A **18**
Forncett St Peter. *Norf*
　—3A **18**
Fornham All Saints. *Suff*
　—3B **24**
Fornham St Martin. *Suff*
　—3B **24**
Forty Hill. *G.Ln* —3A **38**
Forward Green. *Suff* —1D **33**
Fosdyke. *Linc* —2A **6**
Foster Street. *Essx* —3B **38**
Foston. *Linc* —1A **4**
Fotheringhay. *Nptn* —3B **12**
Foul Anchor. *Camb* —1B **14**
Foulden. *Norf* —3A **16**
Foulsham. *Norf* —3D **9**
Four Ashes. *Suff* —2D **25**
Four Gotes. *Camb* —1B **14**
Fowlmere. *Camb* —2B **30**

Foxearth. *Essx* —2B **32**
Fox Hatch. *Essx* —3C **39**
Foxley. *Norf* —3D **9**
Fox Street. *Essx* —1D **41**
Foxton. *Camb* —2B **30**
Framingham Earl. *Norf*
　—2B **18**
Framingham Pigot. *Norf*
　—2B **18**
Framlingham. *Suff* —3B **26**
Frampton. *Linc* —2A **6**
Frampton West End. *Linc*
　—1D **5**
Framsden. *Suff* —1A **34**
Frankfort. *Norf* —3C **11**
Frating Green. *Essx* —1D **41**
Freckenham. *Suff* —2D **23**
Freethorpe. *Norf* —2D **19**
Freiston. *Linc* —1A **6**
Freiston Shore. *Linc* —1A **6**
Frenze. *Norf* —1A **26**
Fressingfield. *Suff* —2B **26**
Freston. *Suff* —3A **34**
Frettenham. *Norf* —1B **18**
Friday Bridge. *Camb* —2B **14**
Frieston. *Linc* —1A **4**
Fring. *Norf* —2A **8**
Frinton-on-Sea. *Essx* —1B **42**
Friston. *Suff* —3D **27**
Frith Bank. *Linc* —1A **6**
Frithsden. *Hert* —3B **36**
Frithville. *Linc* —1A **6**
Fritton. *Norf* —2D **19**
　(nr. Great Yarmouth)
Fritton. *Norf* —3B **18**
　(nr. Long Stratton)
Frogmore. *Hert* —3C **37**
Frognall. *Linc* —1C **13**
Frogshall. *Norf* —2B **10**
Froxfield. *Beds* —3A **28**
Fryerning. *Essx* —3D **39**
Fulbeck. *Linc* —1A **4**
Fulbourn. *Camb* —1C **31**
Fuller Street. *Essx* —2A **40**
Fulmodestone. *Norf* —2C **9**
Fulney. *Linc* —3D **5**
Fundenhall. *Norf* —3A **18**
Furneux Pelham. *Hert*
　—1B **38**
Fyfield. *Essx* —3C **39**

Gainsborough. *Suff* —2A **34**
Gainsford End. *Essx* —3A **32**
Galleyend. *Essx* —3A **40**
Galleywood. *Essx* —3A **40**
Gamlingay. *Camb* —1D **29**
Gamlingay Cinques. *Camb*
　—1D **29**
Gamlingay Great Heath. *Camb*
　—1D **29**
Garboldisham. *Norf* —1D **25**
Garnsgate. *Linc* —3B **6**
Garvestone. *Norf* —2D **17**
Garwick. *Linc* —1C **5**
Gasthorpe. *Norf* —1C **25**
Gateley. *Norf* —3C **9**
Gaultree. *Norf* —2B **14**
Gay Bowers. *Essx* —3A **40**
Gayhurst. *Buck* —2A **28**
Gayton. *Norf* —1A **16**
Gayton Thorpe. *Norf* —1A **16**
Gaywood. *Norf* —3D **7**
Gazeley. *Suff* —3A **24**
Gedding. *Suff* —1C **33**
Geddington. *Nptn* —1A **20**
Gedney. *Linc* —3B **6**

Gedney Broadgate. *Linc*
　—3B
Gedney Drove End. *Linc*
　—3B
Gedney Dyke. *Linc* —3B **6**
Gedney Hill. *Linc* —1A **14**
Geeston. *Leic* —2A **12**
Geldeston. *Norf* —3C **19**
Gelston. *Linc* —1A **4**
Gestingthorpe. *Essx* —3B **32**
Gibraltar. *Suff* —1A **34**
Gillingham. *Norf* —3D **19**
Gimingham. *Norf* —2B **10**
Gipping. *Suff* —3D **25**
Gipsey Bridge. *Linc* —1D **5**
Girton. *Camb* —3B **22**
Gisleham. *Suff* —1D **27**
Gislingham. *Suff* —2D **25**
Gissing. *Norf* —1A **26**
Glandford. *Norf* —1D **9**
Glapthorn. *Nptn* —3B **12**
Glaston. *Leic* —2A **12**
Glatton. *Camb* —1C **21**
Glemsford. *Suff* —2B **32**
Glinton. *Camb* —2C **13**
Goddard's Corner. *Suff*
　—3B **2**
Godmanchester. *Camb*
　—2D **2**
Goff's Oak. *Hert* —3A **38**
Goldhanger. *Essx* —3C **41**
Gold Hill. *Norf* —3C **15**
Goldington. *Beds* —1B **28**
Gonerby Hill Foot. *Linc* —2A
Good Easter. *Essx* —2D **39**
Gooderstone. *Norf* —2A **16**
Gorefield. *Camb* —1B **14**
Gorleston-on-Sea. *Norf*
　—2D **1**
Gosbeck. *Suff* —1A **34**
Gosberton. *Linc* —2D **5**
Gosberton Clough. *Linc*
　—3C
Gosfield. *Essx* —1A **40**
Gosmore. *Hert* —1C **37**
Graby. *Linc* —3B **4**
Grafham. *Camb* —3C **21**
Grafton Underwood. *Nptn*
　—1A **2**
Grantchester. *Camb* —1B **30**
Grantham. *Linc* —2A **4**
Graveley. *Camb* —3D **21**
Graveley. *Hert* —1D **37**
Great Abington. *Camb*
　—2C **3**
Great Addington. *Nptn*
　—2A **2**
Great Amwell. *Hert* —2A **38**
Great Ashfield. *Suff* —3C **25**
Great Baddow. *Essx* —3A **40**
Great Bardfield. *Essx* —3D **3**
Great Barford. *Beds* —1C **29**
Great Barton. *Suff* —3B **24**
Great Bealings. *Suff* —2B **34**
Great Bentley. *Essx* —1A **42**
Great Bircham. *Norf* —2A **8**
Great Blakenham. *Suff*
　—1A **3**
Great Bradley. *Suff* —1D **31**
Great Braxted. *Essx* —2B **40**
Great Bricett. *Suff* —1D **33**
Great Brickhill. *Buck* —3A **28**
Great Bromley. *Essx* —1D **41**
Great Canfield. *Essx* —2C **39**
Great Casterton. *Leic* —2B **1**
Great Chesterford. *Essx*
　—2C **3**

46 East Anglia Regional Atlas

reat Chishill. *Camb* —3B **30**

Great Clacton. *Essx* —2A **42**

reat Cornard. *Suff* —2B **32**

reat Cressingham. *Norf*
—2B **16**

reat Doddington. *Nptn*
—3A **20**

reat Dunham. *Norf* —1B **16**

reat Dunmow. *Essx* —1D **39**

reat Easton. *Essx* —1D **39**

reat Easton. *Leic* —3A **12**

reat Ellingham. *Norf*
—3D **17**

reat Eversden. *Camb*
—1A **30**

reat Finborough. *Suff*
—1D **33**

reatford. *Linc* —1B **12**

reat Fransham. *Norf* —1B **16**

reat Gaddesden. *Hert*
—2B **36**

reat Gidding. *Camb* —1C **21**

reat Glemham. *Suff* —3C **27**

reat Gonerby. *Linc* —2A **4**

reat Gransden. *Camb*
—1D **29**

reat Green. *Norf* —1B **26**

reat Green. *Suff* —1C **33**
(nr. Lavenham)

reat Green. *Suff* —2A **26**
(nr. Palgrave)

reat Hale. *Linc* —1C **5**

reat Hallingbury. *Essx*
—2C **39**

reat Hampden. *Buck*
—3A **36**

reat Harrowden. *Nptn*
—2A **20**

reat Henny. *Essx* —3B **32**

reat Hockham. *Norf* —3C **17**

reat Holland. *Essx* —2B **42**

reat Horkesley. *Essx*
—3C **33**

reat Hormead. *Hert* —3B **30**

reat Leighs. *Essx* —2A **40**

reat Linford. *Buck* —2A **28**

reat Livermere. *Suff* —2B **24**

reat Maplestead. *Essx*
—3B **32**

reat Massingham. *Norf*
—3A **8**

reat Melton. *Norf* —2A **18**

reat Missenden. *Buck*
—3A **36**

reat Moulton. *Norf* —3A **18**

reat Munden. *Hert* —1A **38**

reat Oakley. *Essx* —1A **42**

reat Oakley. *Nptn* —1A **20**

reat Offley. *Hert* —1C **37**

reat Oxney Green. *Essx*
—3D **39**

reat Parndon. *Essx* —3B **38**

reat Paxton. *Camb* —3D **21**

reat Plumstead. *Norf*
—1C **19**

reat Ponton. *Linc* —2A **4**

reat Raveley. *Camb* —1D **21**

reat Ryburgh. *Norf* —3C **9**

reat Saling. *Essx* —1D **39**

reat Sampford. *Essx*
—3D **31**

reat Saxham. *Suff* —3A **24**

reat Shelford. *Camb*
—1B **30**

reat Snoring. *Norf* —2C **9**

reat Staughton. *Camb*
—3C **21**

Great Stukeley. *Camb*
—2D **21**

Great Tey. *Essx* —1B **40**

Great Thurlow. *Suff* —1D **31**

Great Totham North. *Essx*
—2B **40**

Great Totham South. *Essx*
—2B **40**

Great Waldingfield. *Suff*
—2C **33**

Great Walsingham. *Norf*
—2C **9**

Great Waltham. *Essx* —2D **39**

Great Welnetham. *Suff*
—1B **32**

Great Wenham. *Suff* —3D **33**

Great Wigborough. *Essx*
—2C **41**

Great Wilbraham. *Camb*
—1C **31**

Great Witchingham. *Norf*
—1A **18**

Great Wratting. *Suff* —2D **31**

Great Wymondley. *Hert*
—1D **37**

Great Yarmouth. *Norf*
—2D **19**

Great Yeldham. *Essx* —3A **32**

Green End. *Beds* —2B **28**

Green End. *Hert* —3A **30**
(nr. Buntingford)

Green End. *Hert* —1A **38**
(nr. Stevenage)

Greenfield. *Beds* —3B **28**

Greengate. *Norf* —1D **17**

Greensgate. *Norf* —1D **17**

Greenstead Green. *Essx*
—1B **40**

Greensted Green. *Essx*
—3C **39**

Green Street. *Hert* —3C **37**

Green Street. *Suff* —2A **26**

Greenstreet Green. *Suff*
—2D **33**

Green Tye. *Hert* —2B **38**

Greetham. *Leic* —1A **12**

Grendon. *Nptn* —3A **20**

Gresham. *Norf* —2A **10**

Gressenhall. *Norf* —1C **17**

Gretton. *Nptn* —3A **12**

Grimsthorpe. *Linc* —3B **4**

Grimston. *Norf* —3A **8**

Grimstone End. *Suff* —3C **25**

Griston. *Norf* —3C **17**

Gromford. *Suff* —1C **35**

Groton. *Suff* —2C **33**

Grundisburgh. *Suff* —1B **34**

Gubblecote. *Hert* —2A **36**

Guestwick. *Norf* —3D **9**

Guestwick Green. *Norf* —3D **9**

Guilden Morden. *Camb*
—2D **29**

Guist. *Norf* —3C **9**

Gulling Green. *Suff* —1B **32**

Gunby. *Linc* —3A **4**

Gunthorpe. *Camb* —2C **13**

Gunthorpe. *Norf* —2D **9**

Guthram Gowt. *Linc* —3C **5**

Guyhirn. *Camb* —2B **14**

Guyhirn Gull. *Camb* —2A **14**

Guy's Head. *Linc* —3B **6**

Hacconby. *Linc* —3C **5**

Haceby. *Linc* —2B **4**

Hacheston. *Suff* —1C **35**

Hackford. *Norf* —2D **17**

Haddenham. *Camb* —2B **22**

Haddenham End. *Camb*
—2B **22**

Haddiscoe. *Norf* —3D **19**

Haddon. *Camb* —3C **13**

Hadham Cross. *Hert* —2B **38**

Hadham Ford. *Hert* —1B **38**

Hadleigh. *Suff* —2D **33**

Hadleigh Heath. *Suff* —2C **33**

Hadley Wood. *G.Ln* —3D **37**

Hadstock. *Essx* —2C **31**

Hail Weston. *Camb* —3C **21**

Hainford. *Norf* —1B **18**

Hales. *Norf* —3D **19**

Halesgate. *Linc* —3A **6**

Halesworth. *Suff* —2C **27**

Hall End. *Beds* —2B **28**

Halley. *Hert* —2A **38**

Hall Green. *Norf* —1A **26**

Hall's Green. *Hert* —1D **37**

Halltoft End. *Linc* —1A **6**

Halstead. *Essx* —3B **32**

Halton. *Buck* —3A **36**

Halvergate. *Norf* —2D **19**

Hamerton. *Camb* —2C **21**

Hammond Street. *Hert*
—3A **38**

Hamperden End. *Essx*
—3C **31**

Hamrow. *Norf* —3C **9**

Hanby. *Linc* —2B **4**

Hanscombe End. *Beds*
—3C **29**

Hanthorpe. *Linc* —3B **4**

Hanworth. *Norf* —2A **10**

Happisburgh. *Norf* —2C **11**

Happisburgh Common. *Norf*
—3C **11**

Hapton. *Norf* —3A **18**

Hardingham. *Norf* —2D **17**

Hardley Street. *Norf* —2C **19**

Hardmead. *Buck* —2A **28**

Hardwick. *Camb* —1A **30**

Hardwick. *Norf* —1B **26**

Hardwick. *Nptn* —3A **20**

Hardy's Green. *Essx* —1C **41**

Hare Green. *Essx* —1D **41**

Hare Street. *Essx* —3B **38**

Hare Street. *Hert* —1A **38**

Hargate. *Norf* —3A **18**

Hargrave. *Nptn* —2B **20**

Hargrave. *Suff* —1A **32**

Harkstead. *Suff* —3A **34**

Harlaxton. *Linc* —2A **4**

Harleston. *Norf* —1B **26**

Harleston. *Suff* —3D **25**

Harling Road. *Norf* —1C **25**

Harlington. *Beds* —3B **28**

Harlow. *Essx* —3B **38**

Harlton. *Camb* —1A **30**

Harmer Green. *Hert* —2D **37**

Harpenden. *Hert* —2C **37**

Harpley. *Norf* —3A **8**

Harringworth. *Nptn* —3A **12**

Harrold. *Beds* —1A **28**

Harrowden. *Beds* —2B **28**

Harston. *Camb* —1B **30**

Harston. *Leic* —2A **4**

Hartest. *Suff* —1B **32**

Hartford. *Camb* —2D **21**

Hartford End. *Essx* —2D **39**

Harwich. *Essx* —3B **34**

Hasketon. *Suff* —1B **34**

Haslingfield. *Camb* —1B **30**

Hassingham. *Norf* —2C **19**

Hastingwood. *Essx* —3B **38**

Hastoe. *Hert* —3A **36**

Hatch. *Beds* —2C **29**

Hatching Green. *Hert* —2C **37**

Hatfield. *Hert* —3D **37**

Hatfield Broad Oak. *Essx*
—2C **39**

Hatfield Heath. *Essx* —2C **39**

Hatfield Nyde. *Hert* —2D **37**

Hatfield Peverel. *Essx*
—2A **40**

Hatley St George. *Camb*
—1D **29**

Haughley. *Suff* —3D **25**

Haughley Green. *Suff* —3D **25**

Haultwick. *Hert* —1A **38**

Hauxton. *Camb* —1B **30**

Haven Bank. *Linc* —1D **5**

Haverhill. *Suff* —2D **31**

Haverscroft Street. *Norf*
—3D **17**

Hawes Green. *Norf* —3B **18**

Hawkedon. *Suff* —1A **32**

Hawstead. *Suff* —1B **32**

Hawthorpe. *Linc* —3B **4**

Hay Green. *Norf* —1C **15**

Haynes. *Beds* —2B **28**

Haynes West End. *Beds*
—2B **28**

Hay Street. *Hert* —1A **38**

Hazeleigh. *Essx* —3B **40**

Heacham. *Norf* —2D **7**

Heath and Reach. *Beds*
—1A **36**

Heath, The. *Norf* —3B **10**
(nr. Buxton)

Heath, The. *Norf* —3C **9**
(nr. Fakenham)

Heath, The. *Norf* —3A **10**
(nr. Heavingham)

Heath, The. *Suff* —3A **34**

Hebing End. *Hert* —1A **38**

Heckfield Green. *Suff* —2A **26**

Heckfordbridge. *Essx* —1C **41**

Heckington. *Linc* —1C **5**

Hedenham. *Norf* —3C **19**

Helhoughton. *Norf* —3B **8**

Helions Bumpstead. *Essx*
—2D **31**

Hellesdon. *Norf* —1B **18**

Hellington. *Norf* —2C **19**

Helmingham. *Suff* —1A **34**

Helpringham. *Linc* —1C **5**

Helpston. *Camb* —2C **13**

Hemblington. *Norf* —1C **19**

Hemel Hempstead. *Hert*
—3B **36**

Hemingford Abbots. *Camb*
—2D **21**

Hemingford Grey. *Camb*
—2D **21**

Hemingstone. *Suff* —1A **34**

Hemington. *Nptn* —1B **20**

Hemley. *Suff* —2B **34**

Hempnall. *Norf* —3B **18**

Hempnall Green. *Norf*
—3B **18**

Hemp's Green. *Essx* —1C **41**

Hempstead. *Essx* —3D **31**

Hempstead. *Norf* —2A **10**
(nr. Holt)

Hempstead. *Norf* —3D **11**
(nr. Stalham)

Hempton. *Norf* —3C **9**

Hemsby. *Norf* —1D **19**

Hengrave. *Suff* —3B **24**

Henham. *Essx* —1C **39**

Henley. *Suff* —1A **34**

Henlow. *Beds* —3C **29**

Henny Street. *Essx* —3B **32**

Henstead. *Suff* —1D **27**

Hepworth. *Suff* —2C **25**

Herringfleet. *Suff* —3D **19**

Herringswell. *Suff* —3A **24**

Hertford. *Hert* —2A **38**

Hertford Heath. *Hert* —2A **38**

Hertingfordbury. *Hert* —2A **38**

Hessett. *Suff* —3C **25**

Hethersett. *Norf* —2A **18**

Heveningham. *Suff* —2C **27**

Hevingham. *Norf* —3A **10**

Hexton. *Hert* —3C **29**

Heybridge. *Essx* —3D **39**
(nr. Brentwood)

Heybridge. *Essx* —3B **40**
(nr. Maldon)

Heybridge Basin. *Essx*
—3B **40**

Heydon. *Camb* —2B **30**

Heydon. *Norf* —3A **10**

Heydour. *Linc* —2B **4**

Hickling. *Norf* —3D **11**

Hickling Green. *Norf* —3D **11**

Hickling Heath. *Norf* —3D **11**

Higham. *Suff* —3D **33**
(nr. Ipswich)

Higham. *Suff* —3A **24**
(nr. Newmarket)

Higham Ferrers. *Nptn* —3A **20**

Higham Gobion. *Beds*
—3C **29**

High Barnet. *G.Ln* —3D **37**

High Beech. *Essx* —3B **38**

High Common. *Norf* —2C **17**

High Cross. *Hert* —2A **38**

High Easter. *Essx* —2D **39**

High Ferry. *Linc* —1A **6**

Highfields. *Camb* —1A **30**

High Garrett. *Essx* —1A **40**

High Green. *Norf* —2A **18**

High Kelling. *Norf* —1A **10**

High Laver. *Essx* —3C **39**

High Ongar. *Essx* —3C **39**

High Roding. *Essx* —2D **39**

High Street. *Suff* —1D **35**
(nr. Aldeburgh)

High Street. *Suff* —1C **27**
(nr. Bungay)

High Street. *Suff* —2D **27**
(nr. Yoxford)

Highstreet Green. *Essx*
—3A **32**

High Street Green. *Suff*
—1D **33**

Hightown Green. *Suff*
—1C **33**

High Wych. *Hert* —2B **38**

Hilborough. *Norf* —2B **16**

Hildersham. *Camb* —2C **31**

Hilgay. *Norf* —3D **15**

Hilldyke. *Linc* —1A **6**

Hill Green. *Essx* —3B **30**

Hillington. *Norf* —3A **8**

Hilton. *Camb* —3D **21**

Hinderclay. *Suff* —2D **25**

Hindolveston. *Norf* —3D **9**

Hindringham. *Norf* —2C **9**

Hingham. *Norf* —2D **17**

Hintlesham. *Suff* —2D **33**

Hinwick. *Beds* —3A **20**

Hinxton. *Camb* —2B **30**

Hinxworth. *Hert* —2D **29**

Histon. *Camb* —3B **22**

Hitcham. *Suff* —1C **33**

Hitchin. *Hert* —1C **37**

Hobbles Green. *Suff* —1A **32**

Hobbs Cross. *Essx* —3B **38**
Hockering. *Norf* —1D **17**
Hockering Heath. *Norf*
—1D **17**
Hockliffe. *Beds* —1A **36**
Hockwold cum Wilton. *Norf*
—1A **24**
Hoddesdon. *Hert* —3A **38**
Hoe. *Norf* —1C **17**
Hoffleet Stow. *Linc* —2D **5**
Hoggard's Green. *Suff*
—1B **32**
Holbeach. *Linc* —3A **6**
Holbeach Bank. *Linc* —3A **6**
Holbeach Clough. *Linc* —3A **6**
Holbeach Drove. *Linc* —1A **14**
Holbeach Hurn. *Linc* —3A **6**
Holbeach St Johns. *Linc*
—1A **14**
Holbeach St Marks. *Linc*
—2A **6**
Holbeach St Matthew. *Linc*
—2B **6**
Holbrook. *Suff* —3A **34**
Holder's Green. *Essx* —1D **39**
Holdingham. *Linc* —1B **4**
Holkham. *Norf* —1B **8**
Holland Fen. *Linc* —1D **5**
Holland-on-Sea. *Essx* —2A **42**
Hollesley. *Suff* —2C **35**
Hollingdon. *Buck* —1A **36**
Holly End. *Norf* —2B **14**
Holme. *Camb* —1C **21**
Holme Hale. *Norf* —2B **16**
Holme next the Sea. *Norf*
—1A **8**
Holmsey Green. *Suff* —2D **23**
Holt. *Norf* —2D **9**
Holton. *Suff* —2C **27**
Holton St Mary. *Suff* —3D **33**
Holtsmere End. *Hert* —2B **36**
Holwell. *Hert* —3C **29**
Holyfield. *Essx* —3A **38**
Holywell. *Camb* —2A **22**
Holywell Row. *Suff* —2A **24**
Homersfield. *Suff* —1B **26**
Honey Tye. *Suff* —3C **33**
Honing. *Norf* —3C **11**
Honingham. *Norf* —1A **18**
Honington. *Linc* —1A **4**
Honington. *Suff* —2C **25**
Hoo. *Suff* —1B **34**
Hook. *Camb* —3B **14**
Hook's Cross. *Hert* —1D **37**
Hop Pole. *Linc* —1C **13**
Hopton. *Suff* —2C **25**
Hopton on Sea. *Norf* —2D **19**
Horbling. *Linc* —2C **5**
Horham. *Suff* —2B **26**
Horkesley Heath. *Essx*
—1C **41**
Horning. *Norf* —1C **19**
Horningsea. *Camb* —3B **22**
Horningtoft. *Norf* —3C **9**
Horringer. *Suff* —3B **24**
Horseheath. *Camb* —2D **31**
Horseway. *Camb* —1B **22**
Horsey. *Norf* —3D **11**
Horsford. *Norf* —1A **18**
Horsham St Faith. *Norf*
—1B **18**
Horsley Cross. *Essx* —1A **42**
Horsleycross Street. *Essx*
—1A **42**
Horstead. *Norf* —1B **18**
Horton. *Buck* —2A **36**
Hougham. *Linc* —1A **4**

Hough-on-the-Hill. *Linc*
—1A **4**
Houghton. *Camb* —2D **21**
Houghton Conquest. *Beds*
—2B **28**
Houghton Regis. *Beds*
—1B **36**
Houghton St Giles. *Norf*
—2C **9**
Hounslow Green. *Essx*
—2D **39**
Hoveton. *Norf* —1C **19**
Howe. *Norf* —2B **18**
Howe Green. *Essx* —3A **40**
(nr. Chelmsford)
Howegreen. *Essx* —3B **40**
(nr. Maldon)
Howell. *Linc* —1C **5**
How End. *Beds* —2B **28**
Howe Street. *Essx* —2D **39**
(nr. Chelmsford)
Howe Street. *Essx* —3D **31**
(nr. Finchingfield)
How Hill. *Norf* —1C **19**
Howlett End. *Essx* —3C **31**
Hoxne. *Suff* —2A **26**
Hubbert's Bridge. *Linc* —1D **5**
Hulcott. *Buck* —2A **36**
Hulver Street. *Suff* —1D **27**
Humby. *Linc* —2B **4**
Hundle Houses. *Linc* —1D **5**
Hundon. *Suff* —2A **32**
Hungerton. *Linc* —2A **4**
Hunsdon. *Hert* —2B **38**
Hunstanton. *Norf* —1D **7**
Hunston. *Suff* —3C **25**
Huntingdon. *Camb* —2D **21**
Huntingfield. *Suff* —2C **27**
Hunton Bridge. *Hert* —3B **36**
Hunt's Corner. *Norf* —1D **25**
Hunworth. *Norf* —2D **9**
Hurst Green. *Essx* —2D **41**
Husborne Crawley. *Beds*
—3A **28**
Hyde Heath. *Buck* —3A **36**

Ickburgh. *Norf* —3B **16**
Ickleford. *Hert* —3C **29**
Ickleton. *Camb* —2B **30**
Icklingham. *Suff* —2A **24**
Ickwell. *Beds* —2C **29**
Ilketshall St Andrew. *Suff*
—1C **27**
Ilketshall St Lawrence. *Suff*
—1C **27**
Ilketshall St Margaret. *Suff*
—1C **27**
Illington. *Norf* —1C **25**
Impington. *Camb* —3B **22**
Ingatestone. *Essx* —3D **39**
Ingham. *Norf* —3C **11**
Ingham. *Suff* —2B **24**
Ingham Corner. *Norf* —3C **11**
Ingleborough. *Norf* —1B **14**
Ingoldisthorpe. *Norf* —2D **7**
Ingoldsby. *Linc* —2B **4**
Ingthorpe. *Leic* —2A **12**
Ingworth. *Norf* —3A **10**
Intwood. *Norf* —2A **18**
Inworth. *Essx* —2B **40**
Ipswich. *Suff* —2A **34**
Ipswich Airport. *Suff* —2A **34**
Irchester. *Nptn* —3A **20**
Irnham. *Linc* —3B **4**
Iron Bridge. *Camb* —3B **14**

Irstead. *Norf* —3C **11**
Irthlingborough. *Nptn*
—2A **20**
Isham. *Nptn* —2A **20**
Isleham. *Camb* —2D **23**
Islip. *Nptn* —2A **20**
Itteringham. *Norf* —2A **10**
Itteringham Common. *Norf*
—3A **10**
Ivinghoe. *Buck* —2A **36**
Ivinghoe Aston. *Buck* —2A **36**
Ivy Todd. *Norf* —2B **16**
Ixworth. *Suff* —2C **25**
Ixworth Thorpe. *Suff* —2C **25**

Jasper's Green. *Essx* —1A **40**
Jaywick. *Essx* —2A **42**
Jockey End. *Hert* —2B **36**
Johnson's Street. *Norf*
—1C **19**
Jordan Green. *Norf* —3D **9**

Kedington. *Suff* —2A **32**
Keeley Green. *Beds* —2B **28**
Keisby. *Linc* —3B **4**
Kelby. *Linc* —1B **4**
Kelling. *Norf* —1D **9**
Kelsale. *Suff* —3C **27**
Kelshall. *Hert* —3A **30**
Kelvedon. *Essx* —2B **40**
Kelvedon Hatch. *Essx* —3C **39**
Kempston. *Beds* —2B **28**
Kempston Hardwick. *Beds*
—2B **28**
Kennett. *Camb* —3D **23**
Kenninghall. *Norf* —1D **25**
Kennyhill. *Suff* —2D **23**
Kensworth. *Beds* —2B **36**
Kensworth Common. *Beds*
—2B **36**
Kentford. *Suff* —3A **24**
Kenton. *Suff* —3A **26**
Kersey. *Suff* —2D **33**
Kesgrave. *Suff* —2B **34**
Kessingland. *Suff* —1D **27**
Kessingland Beach. *Suff*
—1D **27**
Keswick. *Norf* —2C **11**
(nr. North Walsham)
Keswick. *Norf* —2B **18**
(nr. Norwich)
Kettering. *Nptn* —2A **20**
Ketteringham. *Norf* —2A **18**
Kettlebaston. *Suff* —1C **33**
Kettleburgh. *Suff* —3B **26**
Kettlestone. *Norf* —2C **9**
Ketton. *Leic* —2A **12**
Keysoe. *Beds* —3B **20**
Keysoe Row. *Beds* —3B **20**
Keyston. *Camb* —2B **20**
Kidd's Moor. *Norf* —2A **18**
Kimberley. *Norf* —2D **17**
Kimbolton. *Camb* —3B **20**
Kimpton. *Hert* —2C **37**
Kingsash. *Buck* —3A **36**
King's Cliffe. *Nptn* —3B **12**
Kingshall Street. *Suff* —3C **25**
Kings Langley. *Hert* —3B **36**
King's Lynn. *Norf* —3D **7**
Kings Ripton. *Camb* —2D **21**
Kingston. *Camb* —1A **30**
King's Walden. *Hert* —1C **37**
Kinsbourne Green. *Hert*
—2C **37**
Kirby Bedon. *Norf* —2B **18**

Kirby Cane. *Norf* —3C **19**
Kirby Cross. *Essx* —1B **42**
Kirby le Soken. *Essx* —1B **42**
Kirby Row. *Norf* —3C **19**
Kirkby la Thorpe. *Linc* —1C **5**
Kirkby Underwood. *Linc*
—3B **4**
Kirkley. *Suff* —3D **19**
Kirstead Green. *Norf* —3B **18**
Kirtling. *Camb* —1D **31**
Kirtling Green. *Camb* —1D **31**
Kirton. *Linc* —2A **6**
Kirton. *Suff* —3B **34**
Kirton End. *Linc* —1D **5**
Kirton Holme. *Linc* —1D **5**
Knapton. *Norf* —2C **11**
Knapwell. *Camb* —3A **22**
Knebworth. *Hert* —1D **37**
Kneesworth. *Camb* —2A **30**
Knight's End. *Camb* —3B **14**
Knodishall. *Suff* —3D **27**
Knotting. *Beds* —3B **20**
Knotting Green. *Beds* —3B **20**
Knuston. *Nptn* —3A **20**

Lackford. *Suff* —2A **24**
Lakenham. *Norf* —2B **18**
Lakenheath. *Suff* —1A **24**
Lakesend. *Norf* —3C **15**
Lamarsh. *Essx* —3B **32**
Lamas. *Norf* —3B **10**
Lamb Corner. *Essx* —3D **33**
Landbeach. *Camb* —3B **22**
Langenhoe. *Essx* —2D **41**
Langford. *Beds* —2C **29**
Langford. *Essx* —3B **40**
Langham. *Essx* —3D **33**
Langham. *Leic* —1A **12**
Langham. *Norf* —1D **9**
Langham. *Suff* —3C **25**
Langley. *Essx* —3B **30**
Langley. *Hert* —1D **37**
Langleybury. *Hert* —3B **36**
Langley Green. *Norf* —2C **19**
Langley Street. *Norf* —2C **19**
Langrick. *Linc* —1D **5**
Langriville. *Linc* —1D **5**
Langtoft. *Linc* —1C **13**
Larling. *Norf* —1C **25**
Latchford. *Hert* —1A **38**
Latchingdon. *Essx* —3B **40**
Lathbury. *Buck* —2A **28**
Latimer. *Buck* —3B **36**
Laughton. *Linc* —2B **4**
Lavendon. *Buck* —1A **28**
Lavenham. *Suff* —2C **33**
Lawford. *Essx* —3D **33**
Lawshall. *Suff* —1B **32**
Laxfield. *Suff* —2B **26**
Laxton. *Nptn* —3A **12**
Layer Breton. *Essx* —2C **41**
Layer-de-la-Haye. *Essx*
—1C **41**
Layer Marney. *Essx* —2C **41**
Leadenham. *Linc* —1A **4**
Leaden Roding. *Essx* —2C **39**
Leagrave. *Beds* —1B **36**
Leake Common Side. *Linc*
—1A **6**
Leake Fold Hill. *Linc* —1B **6**
Leake Hurn's End. *Linc*
—1B **6**
Leasingham. *Linc* —1B **4**
Leavenheath. *Suff* —3C **33**
Ledburn. *Buck* —1A **36**
Lee Clump. *Buck* —3A **36**

Lee, The. *Buck* —3A **36**
Leighton Bromswold. *Camb*
—2C **2**
Leighton Buzzard. *Beds*
—1A **3**
Leiston. *Suff* —3D **27**
Lemsford. *Hert* —2D **37**
Lenton. *Linc* —2B **4**
Lenwade. *Norf* —1D **17**
Lessingham. *Norf* —3C **11**
Letchmore Heath. *Hert*
—3C **3**
Letchworth. *Hert* —3D **29**
Letheringham. *Suff* —1B **34**
Letheringsett. *Norf* —2D **9**
Letty Green. *Hert* —2D **37**
Levens Green. *Hert* —1A **38**
Leverington. *Camb* —1B **14**
Leverton. *Linc* —1B **6**
Leverton Lucasgate. *Linc*
—1B **
Leverton Outgate. *Linc* —1B **
Levington. *Suff* —3B **34**
Ley Green. *Hert* —1C **37**
Ley Hill. *Buck* —3A **36**
Leziate. *Norf* —1D **15**
Lidgate. *Suff* —1A **32**
Lidlington. *Beds* —3A **28**
Lilley. *Hert* —1C **37**
Limbury. *Beds* —1B **36**
Limpenhoe. *Norf* —2C **19**
Lindsell. *Essx* —1D **39**
Lindsey. *Suff* —2C **33**
Lindsey Tye. *Suff* —2C **33**
Ling, The. *Norf* —3C **19**
Lingwood. *Norf* —2C **19**
Linslade. *Beds* —1A **36**
Linstead Parva. *Suff* —2C **2**
Linton. *Camb* —2C **31**
Liston. *Essx* —2B **32**
Litcham. *Norf* —1B **16**
Litlington. *Camb* —2A **30**
Little Abington. *Camb*
—2C **
Little Addington. *Nptn*
—2A **
Little Baddow. *Essx* —3A **40**
Little Bardfield. *Essx* —3D **3**
Little Barford. *Beds* —1C **29**
Little Barningham. *Norf*
—2A **
Little Bealings. *Suff* —2B **34**
Little Bentley. *Essx* —1A **42**
Little Berkhampstead. *Hert*
—3D **
Little Billington. *Beds* —1A **
Little Blakenham. *Suff*
—2A **
Little Bradley. *Suff* —1D **31**
Little Brickhill. *Buck* —3A **2**
Little Bromley. *Essx* —1D **4**
Littlebury. *Essx* —3C **31**
Littlebury Green. *Essx*
—3B **
Little Bytham. *Linc* —1B **12**
Little Canfield. *Essx* —1C **39**
Little Casterton. *Leic* —2B **1**
Little Catworth. *Camb* —2C **
Little Chalfont. *Buck* —3A **3**
Little Chesterford. *Essx*
—2C **
Little Chishill. *Camb* —3B **3**
Little Clacton. *Essx* —2A **42**
Little Cornard. *Suff* —3B **32**
Little Crawley. *Buck* —2A **2**
Little Cressingham. *Norf*
—2B **

ttle Ditton. *Camb* —1D **31**
ttle Downham. *Camb*
—1C **23**
ttle Dunham. *Norf* —1B **16**
ttle Dunmow. *Essx* —1D **39**
ttle Easton. *Essx* —1D **39**
ttle Ellingham. *Norf* —3D **17**
ttle End. *Essx* —3C **39**
ttle Eversden. *Camb*
—1A **30**
ttle Fakenham. *Suff* —2C **25**
ttle Fransham. *Norf* —1C **17**
—2A **36**
ttle Gidding. *Camb* —1C **21**
ttle Glemham. *Suff* —1C **35**
ttle Gransden. *Camb*
—1D **29**
ttle Hadham. *Hert* —1B **38**
ttle Hale. *Linc* —1C **5**
ttle Hallingbury. *Essx*
—2B **38**
ttle Hampden. *Buck* —3A **36**
ttle Harrowden. *Nptn*
—2A **20**
ttle Hautbois. *Norf* —3B **10**
ttle Horkesley. *Essx* —3C **33**
ttle Hormead. *Hert* —1B **38**
ttle Irchester. *Nptn* —3A **20**
ttle Laver. *Essx* —3C **39**
ttle Leighs. *Essx* —2A **40**
ttle Linford. *Buck* —2A **28**
ttle London. *Linc* —3B **6**
(nr. Long Sutton)
ttle London. *Linc* —3D **5**
(nr. Spalding)
ttle London. *Norf* —2B **10**
(nr. North Walsham)
ttle London. *Norf* —3A **16**
(nr. Northwold)
ttle London. *Norf* —2A **10**
(nr. Saxthorpe)
ttle London. *Norf* —3D **15**
(nr. Southery)
ttle Maplestead. *Essx*
—3B **32**
ttle Massingham. *Norf*
—3A **8**
ttle Melton. *Norf* —2A **18**
ttle Missenden. *Buck*
—3A **36**
ttle Oakley. *Essx* —1B **42**
ttle Oakley. *Nptn* —1A **20**
ttle Ouse. *Norf* —1D **23**
ttle Paxton. *Camb* —3C **21**
ttle Plumstead. *Norf*
—1C **19**
ttle Ponton. *Linc* —2A **4**
ttleport. *Camb* —1C **23**
ttle Raveley. *Camb* —2D **21**
ttle Ryburgh. *Norf* —3C **9**
ttle Sampford. *Essx*
—3D **31**
ttle Saxham. *Suff* —3A **24**
ttle Shelford. *Camb* —1B **30**
ttle Snoring. *Norf* —2C **9**
ttle Staughton. *Beds*
—3C **21**
ttle Stonham. *Suff* —3A **26**
ttle Street. *Camb* —1C **23**
ttle Stukeley. *Camb* —2D **21**
ttle Sutton. *Linc* —3B **6**
ttle Tey. *Essx* —1B **40**
ttle Thetford. *Camb* —2C **23**
ttle Thurlow. *Suff* —1D **31**
ttle Totham. *Essx* —2B **40**
ttle Walden. *Essx* —2C **31**

Little Waldingfield. *Suff*
—2C **33**
Little Walsingham. *Norf*
—2C **9**
Little Waltham. *Essx* —2A **40**
Little Welnetham. *Suff*
—1B **32**
Little Wenham. *Suff* —3D **33**
Little Whittingham Green. *Suff*
—2B **26**
Little Wilbraham. *Camb*
—1C **31**
Little Wisbeach. *Linc* —2C **5**
Littleworth. *Beds* —2B **28**
Little Wratting. *Suff* —2D **31**
Little Wymington. *Nptn*
—3A **20**
Little Wymondley. *Hert*
—1D **37**
Little Yeldham. *Essx* —3A **32**
Littley Green. *Essx* —2D **39**
Loddon. *Norf* —3C **19**
Lode. *Camb* —3C **23**
Lolworth. *Camb* —3A **22**
London Colney. *Hert* —3C **37**
London Stansted Airport. *Essx*
—1C **39**
Londonthorpe. *Linc* —2A **4**
Long Gardens. *Essx* —3B **32**
Longham. *Norf* —1C **17**
Long Marston. *Hert* —2A **36**
Long Meadow. *Camb* —3C **23**
Long Melford. *Suff* —2B **32**
Longstanton. *Camb* —3A **22**
Longstowe. *Camb* —1A **30**
Long Stratton. *Norf* —3A **18**
Long Sutton. *Linc* —3B **6**
Longthorpe. *Camb* —3C **13**
Long Thurlow. *Suff* —3D **25**
Loosegate. *Linc* —3A **6**
Lound. *Linc* —1B **12**
Lound. *Suff* —3D **19**
Loves Green. *Essx* —3D **39**
Lower Benefield. *Nptn*
—1A **20**
Lower Dean. *Beds* —2B **20**
Lower East Carleton. *Norf*
—2A **18**
Lower End. *Nptn* —3A **20**
Lower Gravenhurst. *Beds*
—3C **29**
Lower Green. *Essx* —3B **30**
Lower Green. *Norf* —2C **9**
Lower Holbrook. *Suff* —3A **34**
Lower Layham. *Suff* —2D **33**
Lower Nazeing. *Essx* —3A **38**
Lower Raydon. *Suff* —3D **33**
Lower Shelton. *Beds* —2A **28**
Lower Stow Bedon. *Norf*
—3C **17**
Lower Street. *Norf* —2B **10**
Lower Sundon. *Beds* —1B **36**
Lower Thurlton. *Norf* —3D **19**
Lowestoft. *Suff* —3D **19**
Low Fulney. *Linc* —3D **5**
Lowick. *Nptn* —1A **20**
Low Street. *Norf* —2D **17**
Luddington in the Brook. *Nptn*
—1C **21**
Ludham. *Norf* —1C **19**
Luffenhall. *Hert* —1D **37**
Lundy Green. *Norf* —3B **18**
Luton. *Beds* —1B **36**
Luton (London) Airport. *Beds*
—1C **37**
Lutton. *Linc* —3B **6**
Lutton. *Nptn* —1C **21**

Lutton Gowts. *Linc* —3B **6**
Lyddington. *Leic* —3A **12**
Lye Green. *Buck* —3A **36**
Lynch Green. *Norf* —2A **18**
Lyndon. *Leic* —2A **12**
Lyng. *Norf* —1D **17**
Lyngate. *Norf* —2B **10**
(nr. North Walsham)
Lyngate. *Norf* —3C **11**
(nr. Worstead)

Mackerye End. *Hert* —2C **37**
Madingley. *Camb* —3A **22**
Magdalen Laver. *Essx*
—3C **39**
Magpie Green. *Suff* —2D **25**
Maldon. *Essx* —3B **40**
Mallows Green. *Essx* —1B **38**
Manea. *Camb* —1B **22**
Manningtree. *Essx* —3A **34**
Manthorpe. *Linc* —2A **4**
(nr. Grantham)
Manthorpe. *Linc* —1B **12**
(nr. Bourne)
Manton. *Leic* —2A **12**
Manuden. *Essx* —1B **38**
March. *Camb* —3B **14**
Margaret Roding. *Essx*
—2C **39**
Margaretting. *Essx* —3D **39**
Margaretting Tye. *Essx*
—3D **39**
Marham. *Norf* —2A **16**
Marholm. *Camb* —2C **13**
Market Deeping. *Linc* —1C **13**
Market Overton. *Leic* —1A **12**
Market Weston. *Suff* —2C **25**
Marks Tey. *Essx* —1C **41**
Markyate. *Hert* —2B **36**
Marlesford. *Suff* —1C **35**
Marlingford. *Norf* —2A **18**
Marshalswick. *Hert* —3C **37**
Marsham. *Norf* —3A **10**
Marsh Side. *Norf* —1A **8**
Marston. *Nott* —1A **4**
Marston Moretaine. *Beds*
—2A **28**
Marsworth. *Buck* —2A **36**
Martham. *Norf* —1D **19**
Martlesham. *Suff* —2B **34**
Martlesham Heath. *Suff*
—2B **34**
Mashbury. *Essx* —2D **39**
Matching. *Essx* —2C **39**
Matching Green. *Essx*
—2C **39**
Matching Tye. *Essx* —2C **39**
Matlaske. *Norf* —2A **10**
Mattishall. *Norf* —1D **17**
Mattishall Burgh. *Norf*
—1D **17**
Maulden. *Beds* —3B **28**
Mautby. *Norf* —1D **19**
Maxey. *Camb* —2C **13**
Mayland. *Essx* —3C **41**
Maylandsea. *Essx* —3C **41**
Maypole Green. *Norf* —3D **19**
Maypole Green. *Suff* —1C **33**
Meesden. *Hert* —3B **30**
Meeting Green. *Suff* —1A **32**
Melbourn. *Camb* —2A **30**
Melchbourne. *Beds* —3B **20**
Meldreth. *Camb* —2A **30**
Mellis. *Suff* —2D **25**
Melton. *Suff* —1B **34**
Melton Constable. *Norf* —2D **9**

Mendham. *Suff* —1B **26**
Mendlesham. *Suff* —3A **26**
Mendlesham Green. *Suff*
—3D **25**
Mentmore. *Buck* —2A **36**
Mepal. *Camb* —1B **22**
Meppershall. *Beds* —3C **29**
Merton. *Norf* —3C **17**
Messing. *Essx* —2B **40**
Metfield. *Suff* —1B **26**
Methwold. *Norf* —3A **16**
Methwold Hythe. *Norf*
—3A **16**
Mettingham. *Suff* —3C **19**
Metton. *Norf* —2A **10**
Mickfield. *Suff* —3A **26**
Micklefield Green. *Hert*
—3B **36**
Mickley Green. *Suff* —1B **32**
Middle Harling. *Norf* —1C **25**
Middleton. *Essx* —3B **32**
Middleton. *Norf* —1D **15**
Middleton. *Nptn* —3A **12**
Middleton. *Suff* —3D **27**
Middlewood Green. *Suff*
—3D **25**
Milden. *Suff* —2C **33**
Mildenhall. *Suff* —2A **24**
Mile End. *Camb* —1D **23**
Mile End. *Essx* —1C **41**
Mileham. *Norf* —1C **17**
Millbrook. *Beds* —3B **28**
Mill Common. *Suff* —1D **27**
Mill End. *Camb* —1D **31**
Mill End. *Hert* —3A **30**
Millfield. *Camb* —3C **13**
Mill Green. *Norf* —1A **26**
Mill Green. *Suff* —2C **33**
Mill Greep. *Essx* —3D **39**
Millow. *Beds* —2D **29**
Mill Street. *Norf* —1D **17**
(nr. Lyng)
Mill Street. *Norf* —1D **17**
(nr. Swanton Morley)
Mill Street. *Suff* —2D **25**
Millthorpe. *Linc* —2C **5**
Milton. *Camb* —3B **22**
Milton Bryan. *Beds* —3A **28**
Milton Ernest. *Beds* —1B **28**
Milton Keynes. *Buck* —3A **28**
Milton Keynes Village. *Buck*
—3A **28**
Mistley. *Essx* —3A **34**
Mistley Heath. *Essx* —3A **34**
Moats Tye. *Suff* —1D **33**
Mogerhanger. *Beds* —2C **29**
Molehill Green. *Essx* —1C **39**
Molesworth. *Camb* —2B **20**
Monewden. *Suff* —1B **34**
Monken Hadley. *G.Ln*
—3D **37**
Monks Eleigh. *Suff* —2C **33**
Monk Soham. *Suff* —3B **26**
Monk Soham Green. *Suff*
—3B **26**
Monk Street. *Essx* —1D **39**
Morborne. *Camb* —3C **13**
Morcott. *Leic* —2A **12**
Morely St Botolph. *Norf*
—3D **17**
Moreton. *Essx* —3C **39**
Morningthorpe. *Norf* —3B **18**
Morris Green. *Essx* —3A **32**
Morston. *Norf* —1D **9**
Morton. *Linc* —3B **4**
Morton. *Norf* —1A **18**
Moulsoe. *Buck* —2A **28**

Moulton. *Linc* —3A **6**
Moulton. *Suff* —3D **23**
Moulton Chapel. *Linc* —1D **13**
Moulton Eugate. *Linc* —1D **13**
Moulton St Mary. *Norf*
—2C **19**
Moulton Seas End. *Linc*
—3A **6**
Mount Bures. *Essx* —3C **33**
Mountnessing. *Essx* —3D **39**
Mount Pleasant. *Norf* —3C **17**
Much Hadham. *Hert* —2B **38**
Muckleton. *Norf* —2B **8**
Mulbarton. *Norf* —2A **18**
Mundesley. *Norf* —2C **11**
Mundford. *Norf* —3B **16**
Mundham. *Norf* —3C **19**
Mundon. *Essx* —3B **40**
Murrow. *Camb* —2A **14**
Mutford. *Suff* —1D **27**

Nacton. *Suff* —2B **34**
Narborough. *Norf* —1A **16**
Nash Lee. *Buck* —3A **36**
Nassington. *Nptn* —3B **12**
Nasty. *Hert* —1A **38**
Naughton. *Suff* —2D **33**
Navestock. *Essx* —3C **39**
Navestock Side. *Essx* —3C **39**
Nayland. *Suff* —3C **33**
Nazeing. *Essx* —3B **38**
Neatishead. *Norf* —3C **11**
Neaton. *Norf* —2C **17**
Necton. *Norf* —2B **16**
Nedging. *Suff* —2D **33**
Nedging Tye. *Suff* —2D **33**
Needham. *Norf* —1B **26**
Needham Market. *Suff*
—1D **33**
Needham Street. *Suff* —3A **24**
Needingworth. *Camb* —2A **22**
Nene Terrace. *Linc* —2D **13**
Nethergate. *Norf* —3D **9**
Nether Street. *Essx* —2C **39**
Nettleden. *Hert* —2B **36**
Newark. *Camb* —2D **13**
Newborough. *Camb* —2D **13**
Newbourne. *Suff* —2B **34**
New Buckenham. *Norf*
—3D **17**
New Costessey. *Norf* —1A **18**
New England. *Camb* —2C **13**
New England. *Essx* —2A **32**
Newgate. *Norf* —1D **9**
Newgate Street. *Hert* —3A **38**
New Greens. *Hert* —3C **37**
New Hainford. *Norf* —1B **18**
New Holkham. *Norf* —2B **8**
New Houghton. *Norf* —3A **8**
Newman's Green. *Suff*
—2B **32**
Newmarket. *Suff* —3D **23**
New Mill. *Hert* —2A **36**
New Mistley. *Essx* —3A **34**
Newnham. *Camb* —1B **30**
Newnham. *Hert* —3D **29**
Newport. *Essx* —3C **31**
Newport. *Norf* —1D **19**
Newport Pagnell. *Buck*
—2A **28**
New Rackheath. *Norf* —1B **18**
Newton. *Camb* —2B **30**
(nr. Cambridge)
Newton. *Camb* —1B **14**
(nr. Wisbech)
Newton. *Linc* —2B **4**

ooksey Green. *Suff* —1C **33**
ootham's Green. *Beds*
—1C **29**
opsley. *Linc* —2A **4**
ose Green. *Essx* —1B **40**
ose Green. *Suff* —2C **33**
otten End. *Suff* —3C **27**
otten Row. *Norf* —1D **17**
ougham. *Norf* —3B **8**
ougham. *Suff* —3C **25**
oughton. *Norf* —2B **10**
oundbush Green. *Essx*
—2C **39**
ow Green. *Essx* —1A **40**
ow Heath. *Essx* —2A **42**
owhedge. *Essx* —1D **41**
owsham. *Buck* —2A **36**
oxton. *Beds* —1C **29**
oxwell. *Essx* —3D **39**
oydon. *Essx* —2B **38**
oydon. *Norf* —1D **25**
(nr. Diss)
oydon. *Norf* —3A **8**
(nr. King's Lynn)
oydon Hamlet. *Essx* —3B **38**
oyston. *Hert* —2A **30**
ucklers Lane. *Hert* —3B **36**
udley Green. *Essx* —3B **40**
umburgh. *Suff* —1C **27**
uncton Holme. *Norf* —2D **15**
unhall. *Norf* —2D **17**
unham. *Norf* —1D **19**
ushall. *Norf* —1A **26**
ushbrooke. *Suff* —3B **24**
ushden. *Hert* —3A **30**
ushden. *Nptn* —3A **20**
ushford. *Suff* —1C **25**
ush Green. *Hert* —1D **37**
ushmere. *Suff* —1D **27**
ushmere St Andrew. *Suff*
—2A **34**
ushton. *Nptn* —1A **20**
uskington. *Linc* —1B **4**
ussel's Green. *Suff* —2B **26**
yhall. *Leic* —1B **12**

acombe. *Hert* —2A **38**
addle Bow. *Norf* —1D **15**
aham Hills. *Norf* —2C **17**
aham Toney. *Norf* —2B **16**
t Albans. *Hert* —3C **37**
t Cross South Elmham. *Suff*
—1B **26**
t Ippollitts. *Hert* —1C **37**
t Ives. *Camb* —2A **22**
t James South Elmham. *Suff*
—1C **27**
t John's Fen End. *Norf*
—1C **15**
t Lawrence. *Essx* —3C **41**
t Leonards. *Buck* —3A **36**
t Margaret's. *Hert* —2B **36**
(nr. Hemel Hempstead)
t Margarets. *Hert* —2A **38**
(nr. Hoddesdon)
t Margaret South Elmham.
Suff —1C **27**
t Michael South Elmham.
Suff —1C **27**
t Neots. *Camb* —3C **21**
t Nicholas South Elmham.
Suff —1C **27**
t Olaves. *Norf* —3D **19**
t Osyth. *Essx* —2A **42**
t Osyth Heath. *Essx* —2A **42**

St Paul's Walden. *Hert*
—1C **37**
Salcott. *Essx* —2C **41**
Salford. *Beds* —3A **28**
Salhouse. *Norf* —1C **19**
Salle. *Norf* —3A **10**
Salph End. *Beds* —1B **28**
Saltby. *Leic* —3A **4**
Salters Lode. *Norf* —2C **15**
Salthouse. *Norf* —1D **9**
Sandhill. *Camb* —1C **23**
Sandholme. *Linc* —2A **6**
Sandon. *Essx* —3A **40**
Sandon. *Hert* —3A **30**
Sandridge. *Hert* —2C **37**
Sandringham. *Norf* —3D **7**
Sandy. *Beds* —2C **29**
Santon Downham. *Suff*
—1B **24**
Sapiston. *Suff* —2C **25**
Sapley. *Camb* —2D **21**
Sapperton. *Linc* —2B **4**
Saracen's Head. *Linc* —3A **6**
Sarratt. *Hert* —3B **36**
Sawbridgeworth. *Hert*
—2B **38**
Sawston. *Camb* —2B **30**
Sawtry. *Camb* —1C **21**
Saxham Street. *Suff* —3D **25**
Saxlingham. *Norf* —2D **9**
Saxlingham Green. *Norf*
—3B **18**
Saxlingham Nethergate. *Norf*
—3B **18**
Saxlingham Thorpe. *Norf*
—3B **18**
Saxmundham. *Suff* —3C **27**
Saxon Street. *Camb* —1D **31**
Saxtead. *Suff* —3B **26**
Saxtead Green. *Suff* —3B **26**
Saxthorpe. *Norf* —2A **10**
Scarning. *Norf* —1C **17**
School Green. *Essx* —3A **32**
Scole. *Norf* —2A **26**
Sco Ruston. *Norf* —3B **10**
Scottlethorpe. *Linc* —3A **4**
Scottow. *Norf* —3B **10**
Scoulton. *Norf* —2C **17**
Scrane End. *Linc* —1A **6**
Scratby. *Norf* —1D **19**
Scredington. *Linc* —1B **4**
Sculthorpe. *Norf* —2B **8**
Seadyke. *Linc* —2A **6**
Sea Palling. *Norf* —3D **11**
Seaton. *Leic* —3A **12**
Seawick. *Essx* —2A **42**
Sedgebrook. *Linc* —2A **4**
Sedgeford. *Norf* —2A **8**
Seething. *Norf* —3C **19**
Semer. *Suff* —2D **33**
Serpentine Green. *Camb*
—3C **13**
Setchey. *Norf* —1D **15**
Sewards End. *Essx* —3C **31**
Sewardstone. *Essx* —3A **38**
Sewell. *Beds* —1A **36**
Sewstern. *Leic* —3A **4**
Shadingfield. *Suff* —1D **27**
Shadwell. *Norf* —1C **25**
Shalford. *Essx* —1A **40**
Shalford Green. *Essx* —1A **40**
Sharnbrook. *Beds* —1A **28**
Sharpenhoe. *Beds* —3B **28**
Sharp Street. *Norf* —3C **11**
Sharrington. *Norf* —2D **9**
Shefford. *Beds* —3C **29**

Shelfanger. *Norf* —1A **26**
Shelley. *Suff* —3D **33**
Shellow Bowells. *Essx*
—3D **39**
Shelton. *Beds* —3B **20**
Shelton. *Norf* —3B **18**
Shelton Green. *Norf* —3B **18**
Shenley. *Hert* —3C **37**
Shenleybury. *Hert* —3C **37**
Shepeau Stow. *Linc* —1A **14**
Shephall. *Hert* —1D **37**
Shepherds Gate. *Norf*
—1C **15**
Shepherd's Port. *Norf* —2D **7**
Shepreth. *Camb* —2A **30**
Shereford. *Norf* —3B **8**
Sheringham. *Norf* —1A **10**
Sherington. *Buck* —2A **28**
Shernborne. *Norf* —2A **8**
Shillington. *Beds* —3C **29**
Shimpling. *Norf* —1A **26**
Shimpling. *Suff* —1B **32**
Shimpling Street. *Suff*
—1B **32**
Shingay. *Camb* —2A **30**
Shingham. *Norf* —2A **16**
Shingle Street. *Suff* —2C **35**
Shipdham. *Norf* —2C **17**
Shipmeadow. *Suff* —3C **19**
Shop Street. *Suff* —3B **26**
Short Green. *Norf* —1D **25**
Shortstown. *Beds* —2B **28**
Shotesham. *Norf* —3B **18**
Shotley. *Suff* —3B **34**
Shotley Gate. *Suff* —3B **34**
Shottisham. *Suff* —2C **35**
Shouldham. *Norf* —2D **15**
Shouldham Thorpe. *Norf*
—2D **15**
Shropham. *Norf* —3C **17**
Shrub End. *Essx* —1C **41**
Shudy Camps. *Camb* —2D **31**
Sible Hedingham. *Essx*
—3A **32**
Sibsey. *Linc* —1A **6**
Sibsey Fen Side. *Linc* —1A **6**
Sibson. *Camb* —3B **12**
Sibton. *Suff* —3C **27**
Sicklesmere. *Suff* —3B **24**
Sidestrand. *Norf* —2B **10**
Silfield. *Norf* —3A **18**
Silk Willoughby. *Linc* —1B **4**
Silsoe. *Beds* —3B **28**
Silver End. *Essx* —2B **40**
Silvergate. *Norf* —3A **10**
Silverley's Green. *Suff*
—2B **26**
Six Mile Bottom. *Camb*
—1C **31**
Sizewell. *Suff* —3D **27**
Skeldyke. *Linc* —2A **6**
Skeyton. *Norf* —3B **10**
Skeyton Corner. *Norf* —3B **10**
Skillington. *Linc* —3A **4**
Skirbeck. *Linc* —1A **6**
Skirbeck Quarter. *Linc* —1A **6**
Skye Green. *Essx* —1B **40**
Slade Field. *Camb* —1A **22**
Slapton. *Buck* —1A **36**
Sleaford. *Linc* —1B **4**
Slip End. *Hert* —2B **36**
Slipton. *Nptn* —2A **20**
Sloley. *Norf* —3B **10**
Smallburgh. *Norf* —3C **11**
Smallworth. *Norf* —1D **25**
Smeeth, The. *Norf* —1C **15**
Smith's Green. *Essx* —1C **39**

Smithwood Green. *Suff*
—1C **33**
Smyth's Green. *Essx* —2C **41**
Snailwell. *Camb* —3D **23**
Snape. *Suff* —1C **35**
Snetterton. *Norf* —3C **17**
Snettisham. *Norf* —2D **7**
Snow Street. *Norf* —1D **25**
Soham. *Camb* —2C **23**
Soham Cotes. *Camb* —2C **23**
Somerleyton. *Suff* —3D **19**
Somersham. *Camb* —2A **22**
Somersham. *Suff* —2D **33**
Somerton. *Suff* —1B **32**
Sotterley. *Suff* —1D **27**
Soulbury. *Buck* —1A **36**
Souldrop. *Beds* —3A **20**
South Acre. *Norf* —1B **16**
Southburgh. *Norf* —2C **17**
South Burlingham. *Norf*
—2C **19**
Southcott. *Beds* —1A **36**
South Cove. *Suff* —1D **27**
South Creake. *Norf* —2B **8**
Southery. *Norf* —3D **15**
Southey Green. *Essx* —3A **32**
Southgate. *Norf* —3A **10**
(nr. Aylsham)
Southgate. *Norf* —2D **7**
(nr. Dersingham)
Southgate. *Norf* —2B **8**
(nr. Fakenham)
South Green. *Essx* —2D **41**
South Hanningfield. *Essx*
—3A **40**
South Heath. *Buck* —3A **36**
South Heath. *Essx* —2A **42**
Southill. *Beds* —2C **29**
South Kyme. *Linc* —1C **5**
South Lopham. *Norf* —1D **25**
South Luffenham. *Leic*
—2A **12**
South Mimms. *Hert* —3D **37**
Southminster. *Essx* —3C **41**
Southoe. *Camb* —3C **21**
Southolt. *Suff* —3A **26**
Southorpe. *Camb* —2B **12**
South Pickenham. *Norf*
—2B **16**
South Rauceby. *Linc* —1B **4**
South Raynham. *Norf* —3B **8**
Southrepps. *Norf* —2B **10**
South Runcton. *Norf* —2D **15**
Southtown. *Norf* —2D **19**
South Walsham. *Norf*
—1C **19**
Southwick. *Nptn* —3B **12**
South Witham. *Linc* —1A **12**
Southwold. *Suff* —2D **27**
Southwood. *Norf* —2C **19**
South Woodham Ferrers. *Essx*
—3B **40**
South Wootton. *Norf* —3D **7**
Sowley Green. *Suff* —1A **32**
Spa Common. *Norf* —2B **10**
Spalding. *Linc* —3D **5**
Spaldwick. *Camb* —2C **21**
Spanby. *Linc* —2B **4**
Sparham. *Norf* —1D **17**
Sparhamhill. *Norf* —1D **17**
Sparrow Green. *Norf* —1C **17**
Spellbrook. *Hert* —2B **38**
Spexhall. *Suff* —1C **27**
Spixworth. *Norf* —1B **18**
Spooner Row. *Norf* —3D **17**
Sporle. *Norf* —1B **16**
Sproughton. *Suff* —2A **34**

Sprowston. *Norf* —1B **18**
Sproxton. *Leic* —3A **4**
Stacksford. *Norf* —3D **17**
Stagden Cross. *Essx* —2D **39**
Stagsden. *Beds* —2A **28**
Stainby. *Linc* —3A **4**
Stainfield. *Linc* —3B **4**
Stalham. *Norf* —3C **11**
Stalham Green. *Norf* —3C **11**
Stambourne. *Essx* —3A **32**
Stamford. *Linc* —2B **12**
Stanborough. *Hert* —2D **37**
Stanbridge. *Beds* —1A **36**
Standon. *Hert* —1A **38**
Standon Green End. *Hert*
—2A **38**
Standwell Green. *Suff*
—2A **26**
Stanfield. *Norf* —3C **9**
Stanford. *Beds* —2C **29**
Stanford Rivers. *Essx*
—3C **39**
Stanground. *Camb* —3D **13**
Stanhoe. *Norf* —2B **8**
Stanion. *Nptn* —1A **20**
Stanningfield. *Suff* —1B **32**
Stansfield. *Suff* —1A **32**
Stanstead. *Suff* —2B **32**
Stanstead Abbots. *Hert*
—2A **38**
Stansted (London) Airport.
Essx —1C **39**
Stansted Mountfitchet. *Essx*
—1C **39**
Stanton. *Suff* —2C **25**
Stanton Chare. *Suff* —2C **25**
Stanton Street. *Suff* —3C **25**
Stanway. *Essx* —1C **41**
Stanwick. *Nptn* —2A **20**
Stapleford. *Camb* —1B **30**
Stapleford. *Hert* —2A **38**
Stapleford Tawney. *Essx*
—3C **39**
Staploe. *Beds* —3C **21**
Starling's Green. *Essx*
—3B **30**
Starston. *Norf* —1B **26**
Start Hill. *Essx* —1C **39**
Staughton Green. *Camb*
—3C **21**
Staughton Highway. *Camb*
—3C **21**
Stebbing. *Essx* —1D **39**
Stebbing Green. *Essx*
—1D **39**
Steeple. *Essx* —3C **41**
Steeple Bumpstead. *Essx*
—2D **31**
Steeple Gidding. *Camb*
—1C **21**
Steeple Morden. *Camb*
—2D **23**
Steppingley. *Beds* —3B **28**
Sternfield. *Suff* —3C **27**
Stetchworth. *Camb* —1D **31**
Stevenage. *Hert* —1D **37**
Stevington. *Beds* —1A **28**
Stevington End. *Camb*
—2C **31**
Stewartby. *Beds* —2B **28**
Stewkley. *Buck* —1A **36**
Stibbard. *Norf* —3C **9**
Stibbington. *Camb* —3B **12**
Stickling Green. *Essx* —3B **30**
Stiffkey. *Norf* —1C **9**
Stilton. *Camb* —1C **21**
Stisted. *Essx* —1A **40**

Stock. *Essx* —3D **39**
Stocking Green. *Essx* —3C **31**
Stocking Pelham. *Hert*
—1B **38**
Stockstreet. *Essx* —1B **40**
Stockton. *Norf* —3C **19**
Stody. *Norf* —2D **9**
Stoke Ash. *Suff* —2A **26**
Stoke by Clare. *Suff* —2A **32**
Stoke-by-Nayland. *Suff*
—3C **33**
Stoke Doyle. *Nptn* —1B **20**
Stoke Dry. *Leic* —3A **12**
Stoke Ferry. *Norf* —3A **16**
Stoke Goldington. *Buck*
—2A **28**
Stoke Hammond. *Buck*
—1A **36**
Stoke Holy Cross. *Norf*
—2B **18**
Stoke Rochford. *Linc* —3A **4**
Stokesby. *Norf* —1D **19**
Stondon Massey. *Essx*
—3C **39**
Stonea. *Camb* —3B **14**
Stone Bridge Corner. *Camb*
—2D **13**
Stonely. *Camb* —3C **21**
Stones Green. *Essx* —1A **42**
Stone Street. *Suff* —3C **33**
(nr. Boxford)
Stone Street. *Suff* —1C **27**
(nr. Halesworth)
Stoneyhills. *Essx* —3C **41**
Stonham Aspel. *Suff* —1A **34**
Stopsley. *Buck* —1C **37**
Stotfold. *Beds* —3D **29**
Stoven. *Suff* —1D **27**
Stow. *Linc* —2B **4**
Stow Bardolph. *Norf* —2D **15**
Stow Bedon. *Norf* —3C **17**
Stowbridge. *Norf* —2D **15**
Stow cum Quy. *Camb*
—3C **23**
Stowlangtoft. *Suff* —3C **25**
Stow Longa. *Camb* —2C **21**
Stow Maries. *Essx* —3B **40**
Stowmarket. *Suff* —1D **33**
Stowupland. *Suff* —1D **33**
Stradbroke. *Suff* —2B **26**
Stradishall. *Suff* —1A **32**
Stradsett. *Norf* —2D **15**
Stragglethorpe. *Linc* —1A **4**
Stratford St Andrew. *Suff*
—3C **27**
Stratford St Mary. *Suff*
—3D **33**
Stratton St Michael. *Norf*
—3B **18**
Stratton Strawless. *Norf*
—3B **10**
Streatley. *Beds* —1B **36**
Streetly End. *Camb* —2D **31**
Strethall. *Essx* —3B **30**
Stretham. *Camb* —2C **23**
Stretton. *Leic* —1A **12**
Strixton. *Nptn* —3A **20**
Stroxton. *Linc* —2A **4**
Strugg's Hill. *Linc* —2D **5**
Strumpshaw. *Norf* —2C **19**
Stubbs Green. *Norf* —3C **19**
Stubton. *Linc* —1A **4**
Studham. *Beds* —2B **36**
Stuntney. *Camb* —2C **23**
Sturmer. *Essx* —2D **31**
Stuston. *Suff* —2A **26**
Stutton. *Suff* —3A **34**

Sudborough. *Nptn* —1A **20**
Sudbourne. *Suff* —1D **35**
Sudbrook. *Linc* —1A **4**
Sudbury. *Suff* —2B **32**
Suffield. *Norf* —2B **10**
Summerfield. *Norf* —2A **8**
Sundon Park. *Beds* —1B **36**
Surfleet. *Linc* —3D **5**
Surfleet Seas End. *Linc*
—3D **5**
Surlingham. *Norf* —2C **19**
Surrex. *Essx* —1B **40**
Sustead. *Norf* —2A **10**
Suton. *Norf* —3D **17**
Sutterton. *Linc* —2D **5**
Sutterton Dowdyke. *Linc*
—2D **5**
Sutton. *Beds* —2D **29**
Sutton. *Camb* —2B **22**
(nr. Ely)
Sutton. *Camb* —3B **12**
(nr. Peterborough)
Sutton. *Norf* —3C **11**
Sutton. *Suff* —2C **35**
Sutton Bridge. *Linc* —3B **6**
Sutton Corner. *Linc* —3B **6**
Sutton Crosses. *Linc* —3B **6**
Sutton Gault. *Camb* —2B **22**
Sutton St Edmund. *Linc*
—1A **14**
Sutton St Edmund's Common.
Linc —2A **14**
Sutton St James. *Linc*
—1A **14**
Swaffham. *Norf* —2B **16**
Swaffham Bulbeck. *Camb*
—3C **23**
Swaffham Prior. *Camb*
—3C **23**
Swafield. *Norf* —2B **10**
Swainsthorpe. *Norf* —2B **18**
Swannington. *Norf* —1A **18**
Swan Street. *Essx*. —1B **40**
Swanton Abbot. *Norf* —3B **10**
Swanton Morley. *Norf*
—1D **17**
Swanton Novers. *Norf* —2D **9**
Swarby. *Linc* —1B **4**
Swardeston. *Norf* —2B **18**
Swaton. *Linc* —2C **5**
Swavesey. *Camb* —3A **22**
Swayfield. *Linc* —3A **4**
Swefling. *Suff* —3C **27**
Swilland. *Suff* —1A **34**
Swineshead. *Beds* —3B **20**
Swineshead. *Linc* —1D **5**
Swineshead Bridge. *Linc*
—1D **5**
Swingbrow. *Camb* —1A **22**
Swingleton Green. *Suff*
—2C **33**
Swinstead. *Linc* —3B **4**
Syderstone. *Norf* —2B **8**
Syleham. *Suff* —2B **26**
Syston. *Linc* —1A **4**

Tacolneston. *Norf* —3A **18**
Tadlow. *Camb* —2D **29**
Takeley. *Essx* —1C **39**
Takeley Street. *Essx* —1C **39**
Tallington. *Linc* —2B **12**
Tamworth Green. *Linc* —1A **6**
Tannington. *Suff* —3B **26**
Tan Office Green. *Suff*
—1A **32**
Tansor. *Nptn* —3B **12**

Tasburgh. *Norf* —3B **18**
Tatterford. *Norf* —3B **8**
Tattersett. *Norf* —2B **8**
Tattingstone. *Suff* —3A **34**
Tattingstone White Horse. *Suff*
—3A **34**
Taverham. *Norf* —1A **18**
Taverners Green. *Essx*
—2C **39**
Tebworth. *Beds* —1A **36**
Teigh. *Leic* —1A **12**
Tempsford. *Beds* —1C **29**
Tendring. *Essx* —1A **42**
Tendring Green. *Essx* —1A **42**
Ten Mile Bank. *Norf* —3D **15**
Terling. *Essx* —2A **40**
Terrick. *Buck* —3A **36**
Terrington St Clement. *Norf*
—3C **7**
Terrington St John. *Norf*
—1C **15**
Teversham. *Camb* —1B **30**
Tewin. *Hert* —2D **37**
Tharston. *Norf* —3A **18**
Thaxted. *Essx* —3D **31**
Theberton. *Suff* —3D **27**
Thelnetham. *Suff* —2D **25**
Thelveton. *Norf* —1A **26**
Themelthorpe. *Norf* —3D **9**
Therfield. *Hert* —3A **30**
Thetford. *Linc* —1C **13**
Thetford. *Norf* —1B **24**
Theydon Bois. *Essx* —3B **38**
Thistleton. *Leic* —1A **12**
Thistley Green. *Suff* —2D **23**
Tholomas Drove. *Camb*
—2B **14**
Thompson. *Norf* —3C **17**
Thorington. *Suff* —2D **27**
Thorington Street. *Suff*
—3D **33**
Thorley. *Hert* —2B **38**
Thorley Street. *Hert* —2B **38**
Thornage. *Norf* —2D **9**
Thorncote Green. *Beds*
—2C **29**
Thorndon. *Suff* —3A **26**
Thorney. *Camb* —2D **13**
Thorney Toll. *Camb* —2A **14**
Thornham. *Norf* —1A **8**
Thornham Magna. *Suff*
—2A **26**
Thornham Parva. *Suff*
—2A **26**
Thornhaugh. *Camb* —2B **12**
Thorns. *Suff* —1A **32**
Thornwood Common. *Essx*
—3B **38**
Thorpe. *Norf* —3D **19**
Thorpe Abbotts. *Norf* —2A **26**
Thorpe by Water. *Leic*
—3A **12**
Thorpe Common. *Suff*
—3B **34**
Thorpe End. *Norf* —1B **18**
Thorpe Green. *Essx* —1A **42**
Thorpe Green. *Suff* —1C **33**
Thorpe Hamlet. *Norf* —2B **18**
Thorpe Latimer. *Linc* —1C **5**
Thorpe-le-Soken. *Essx*
—1A **42**
Thorpe Market. *Norf* —2B **10**
Thorpe Marriot. *Norf* —1A **18**
Thorpe Morieux. *Suff* —1C **33**
Thorpeness. *Suff* —3D **27**
Thorpe Waterville. *Nptn*
—1B **20**

Thorpland. *Norf* —2D **15**
Thorrington. *Essx* —1D **41**
Thrandeston. *Suff* —2A **26**
Thrapston. *Nptn* —2A **20**
Three Holes. *Norf* —2C **15**
Threekingham. *Linc* —2B **4**
Thrigby. *Norf* —1D **19**
Thriplow. *Camb* —2B **30**
Throckenholt. *Linc* —2A **14**
Throcking. *Hert* —3A **30**
Thurgarton. *Norf* —2A **10**
Thurlby. *Linc* —1C **13**
Thurleigh. *Beds* —1B **28**
Thurlton. *Norf* —3D **19**
Thurne. *Norf* —1D **19**
Thurning. *Norf* —3D **9**
Thurning. *Nptn* —1B **20**
Thursford. *Norf* —2C **9**
Thursford Green. *Norf* —2C **9**
Thurston. *Suff* —3C **25**
Thurston End. *Suff* —1A **32**
Thurton. *Norf* —2C **19**
Thuxton. *Norf* —2D **17**
Thwaite. *Suff* —3A **26**
Thwaite St Mary. *Norf*
—3C **19**
Tibenham. *Norf* —1A **26**
Tickencote. *Leic* —2A **12**
Tilbrook. *Camb* —3B **20**
Tillingham. *Essx* —3C **41**
Tilney All Saints. *Norf*
—1C **15**
Tilney Fen Side. *Norf* —1C **15**
Tilney High End. *Norf* —1C **15**
Tilney St Lawrence. *Norf*
—1C **15**
Tilsworth. *Beds* —1A **36**
Timworth Green. *Suff*
—3B **24**
Tingrith. *Beds* —3B **28**
Tinwell. *Leic* —2B **12**
Tips End. *Camb & Norf*
—3C **15**
Tiptree. *Essx* —2B **40**
Tiptree Heath. *Essx* —2B **40**
Titchmarsh. *Nptn* —2B **20**
Titchwell. *Norf* —1A **8**
Tittleshall. *Norf* —3B **8**
Tivetshall St Margaret. *Norf*
—1A **26**
Tivetshall St Mary. *Norf*
—1A **26**
Tixover. *Leic* —2A **12**
Toddington. *Beds* —1B **36**
Toft. *Camb* —1A **30**
Toft. *Linc* —1B **12**
Toft Monks. *Norf* —3D **19**
Toftrees. *Norf* —3B **8**
Toftwood. *Norf* —1C **17**
Tollesbury. *Essx* —2C **41**
Tolleshunt D'Arcy. *Essx*
—2C **41**
Tolleshunt Knights. *Essx*
—2C **41**
Tolleshunt Major. *Essx*
—2C **41**
Tonwell. *Hert* —2A **38**
Toot Hill. *Essx* —3C **39**
Topcroft. *Norf* —3B **18**
Topcroft Street. *Norf* —3B **18**
Toppesfield. *Essx* —3A **32**
Toprow. *Norf* —3A **18**
Toseland. *Camb* —3D **21**
Tostock. *Suff* —3C **25**
Tottenhill. *Norf* —1D **15**
Tottenhill Row. *Norf* —1D **15**
Totternhoe. *Beds* —1A **36**

Tower End. *Norf* —1D **15**
Town End. *Camb* —3B **14**
Towngate. *Linc* —1C **13**
Townsend. *Hert* —3C **37**
Town Street. *Suff* —1A **24**
Trimingham. *Norf* —2B **10**
Trimley Lower Street. *Suff*
—3B
Trimley St Martin. *Suff*
—3B
Trimley St Mary. *Suff* —3B
Tring. *Hert* —2A **36**
Troston. *Suff* —2B **24**
Trowley Bottom. *Hert* —2B
Trowse Newton. *Norf* —2B **1**
Trumpington. *Camb* —1B **30**
Trunch. *Norf* —2B **10**
Tuddenham. *Suff* —2A **34**
(nr. Ipswich)
Tuddenham. *Suff* —2A **24**
(nr. Mildenhall)
Tumbler's Green. *Essx*
—1B **4**
Tungate. *Norf* —3B **10**
Tunstall. *Norf* —2D **19**
Tunstall. *Suff* —1C **35**
Tunstead. *Norf* —3B **10**
Turvey. *Beds* —1A **28**
Tuttington. *Norf* —3B **10**
Twenty. *Linc* —3C **5**
Twinstead. *Essx* —3B **32**
Twinstead Green. *Essx*
—3B
Twyford. *Norf* —3D **9**
Twywell. *Nptn* —2A **20**
Tyby. *Norf* —3D **9**
Tydd Gote. *Linc* —1B **14**
Tydd St Giles. *Camb* —1B **1**
Tydd St Mary. *Linc* —1B **14**
Tye Green. *Essx* —1C **39**
(nr. Bishop's Stortford)
Tye Green. *Essx* —1A **40**
(nr. Braintree)
Tye Green. *Essx* —3C **31**
(nr. Saffron Walden)
Tyler's Green. *Essx* —3C **39**
Tyringham. *Buck* —2A **28**

Ubbeston Green. *Suff*
—2C **2**
Uffington. *Linc* —2B **12**
Ufford. *Camb* —2B **12**
Ufford. *Suff* —1B **34**
Uggeshall. *Suff* —2D **27**
Ugley. *Essx* —1C **39**
Ugley Green. *Essx* —1C **39**
Ulting. *Essx* —3B **40**
Undley. *Suff* —1D **23**
Upend. *Camb* —1A **32**
Upgate. *Norf* —1A **18**
Upgate Street. *Norf* —3D **17**
Upper Benefield. *Nptn*
—1A **2**
Upper Caldecote. *Beds*
—2C **2**
Upper Dean. *Beds* —3B **20**
Upper Dovercourt. *Essx*
—3B
Upper Dunsley. *Hert* —2A **3**
Upper Gravenhurst. *Beds*
—3C **2**
Upper Green. *Essx* —3B **30**
Upper Hambleton. *Leic*
—2A **1**
Upper Hellesdon. *Norf*
—1B **1**

Upper Layham. *Suff* —2D **33**
Upper Shelton. *Beds* —2A **28**
Upper Sheringham. *Norf*
—1A **10**
Upper Staploe. *Beds* —1C **29**
Upper Stoke. *Norf* —2B **18**
Upper Stondon. *Beds* —3C **29**
Upper Street. *Norf* —1C **19**
(nr. Horning)
Upper Street. *Norf* —1C **19**
(nr. Hoveton)
Upper Street. *Suff* —3A **34**
Upper Sundon. *Beds* —1B **36**
Uppingham. *Leic* —3A **12**
Upshire. *Essx* —3B **38**
Upthorpe. *Suff* —2C **25**
Upton. *Camb* —2C **21**
(nr. Huntingdon)
Upton. *Camb* —2C **13**
(nr. Peterborough)
Upton. *Norf* —1C **19**
Upton End. *Beds* —3C **29**
Upware. *Camb* —2C **23**
Upwell. *Camb* —2B **14**
Upwick Green. *Hert* —1B **38**
Upwood. *Camb* —1D **21**

Wacton. *Norf* —3A **18**
Wadenhoe. *Nptn* —1B **20**
Wadesmill. *Hert* —2A **38**
Wakerley. *Nptn* —3A **12**
Wakes Colne. *Essx* —1B **40**
Walberswick. *Suff* —2D **27**
Walcot. *Linc* —2B **4**
Walcot Green. *Norf* —1A **26**
Walcott. *Norf* —2C **11**
Waldringfield. *Suff* —2B **34**
Walkern. *Hert* —1D **37**
Wallington. *Hert* —3D **29**
Walpole. *Suff* —2C **27**
Walpole Cross Keys. *Norf*
—1C **15**
Walpole Gate. *Norf* —1C **15**
Walpole Highway. *Norf*
—1C **15**
Walpolelane. *Suff* —2C **27**
Walpole Marsh. *Norf* —1B **14**
Walpole St Andrew. *Norf*
—1C **15**
Walpole St Peter. *Norf*
—1C **15**
Walsham le Willows. *Suff*
—2D **25**
Walsoken. *Camb* —1B **14**
Walsworth. *Hert* —3C **29**
Waltham Abbey. *Essx*
—3A **38**
Waltham Cross. *Hert* —3A **38**
Waltham's Cross. *Essx*
—3D **31**
Walton. *Buck* —3A **28**
Walton. *Camb* —2C **13**
Walton. *Suff* —3B **34**
Walton Highway. *Norf*
—1B **14**
Walton-on-the-Naze. *Essx*
—1B **42**
Wangford. *Suff* —1A **24**
(nr. Lakenheath)
Wangford. *Suff* —2D **27**
(nr. Southwold)
Wansford. *Camb* —3B **12**
Warboys. *Camb* —1A **22**
Ward Green. *Suff* —3D **25**
Wardhedges. *Beds* —3B **28**
Wardy Hill. *Camb* —1B **22**

Ware. *Hert* —2A **38**
Wareside. *Hert* —2A **38**
Waresley. *Camb* —1D **29**
Wargate. *Linc* —2D **5**
Warham. *Norf* —1C **9**
Warkton. *Nptn* —2A **20**
Warmington. *Nptn* —3B **12**
Warners End. *Hert* —3B **36**
Warrington. *Buck* —1A **28**
Washbrook. *Suff* —2A **34**
Waterbeach. *Camb* —3B **22**
Waterden. *Norf* —2B **8**
Water End. *Beds* —3B **28**
Water End. *Hert* —3D **37**
(nr. Hatfield)
Water End. *Hert* —2B **36**
(nr. Hemel Hempstead)
Waterford. *Hert* —2A **38**
Waterloo. *Norf* —1B **18**
Water Newton. *Camb* —3C **13**
Waterside. *Buck* —3A **36**
Waterside. *Camb* —2D **23**
Watford. *Hert* —3B **36**
Watlington. *Norf* —1D **15**
Wattisfield. *Suff* —2D **25**
Wattisham. *Suff* —1D **33**
Watton. *Norf* —2C **17**
Watton at Stone. *Hert*
—2D **37**
Wavendon. *Buck* —3A **28**
Waxham. *Norf* —3D **11**
Way Head. *Camb* —1B **22**
Weasenham All Saints. *Norf*
—3B **8**
Weasenham St Peter. *Norf*
—3B **8**
Weekley. *Nptn* —1A **20**
Weeley. *Essx* —1A **42**
Weeley Heath. *Essx* —1A **42**
Weeting. *Norf* —1A **24**
Welborne. *Norf* —1D **17**
Welby. *Linc* —2A **4**
Welches Dam. *Camb* —1B **22**
Weldon. *Nptn* —1A **20**
Welham Green. *Hert* —3D **37**
Wellingborough. *Nptn*
—3A **20**
Wellingham. *Norf* —3B **8**
Wellpond Green. *Hert* —1B **38**
Wells-next-the-Sea. *Norf*
—1C **9**
Welney. *Norf* —3C **15**
Welwyn. *Hert* —2D **37**
Welwyn Garden City. *Hert*
—2D **37**
Wendens Ambo. *Essx*
—3C **31**
Wending. *Norf* —1C **17**
Wendover. *Buck* —3A **36**
Wendy. *Camb* —2A **30**
Wenhaston. *Suff* —2D **27**
Wennington. *Camb* —2D **21**
Wentworth. *Camb* —2B **22**
Wereham. *Norf* —2D **15**
Werrington. *Camb* —2C **13**
West Acre. *Norf* —1A **16**
West Barsham. *Norf* —2C **9**
West Beckham. *Norf* —2A **10**
West Bergholt. *Essx* —1C **41**
West Bilney. *Norf* —1A **16**
Westborough. *Linc* —1A **4**
West Bradenham. *Norf*
—2C **17**
West Briggs. *Norf* —1D **15**
Westby. *Linc* —3A **4**
West Caister. *Norf* —1D **19**
West Deeping. *Linc* —2C **13**

West Dereham. *Norf* —2D **15**
West End. *Beds* —1A **28**
West End. *Camb* —3B **14**
West End. *Hert* —3D **37**
West End. *Linc* —1A **6**
West End. *Norf* —1D **19**
Westerfield. *Suff* —2A **34**
Westfield. *Norf* —2C **17**
Westgate. *Norf* —1C **9**
Westhall. *Suff* —1D **27**
West Hanningfield. *Essx*
—3A **40**
West Head. *Norf* —2C **15**
Westhorpe. *Linc* —2D **5**
Westhorpe. *Suff* —3D **25**
West Leith. *Hert* —2A **36**
Westleton. *Suff* —3D **27**
West Lexham. *Norf* —1B **16**
Westley. *Suff* —3B **24**
Westley Waterless. *Camb*
—1D **31**
West Lynn. *Norf* —1D **15**
West Mersea. *Essx* —2D **41**
Westmill. *Hert* —1A **38**
(nr. Buntingford)
West Mill. *Hert* —3C **29**
(nr. Hitchin)
West Newton. *Norf* —3D **7**
Weston. *Hert* —3D **29**
Weston. *Linc* —3D **5**
Weston Colville. *Camb*
—1D **31**
Weston Ditch. *Suff* —2D **23**
Weston Green. *Camb* —1D **31**
Weston Green. *Norf* —1A **18**
Weston Hills. *Linc* —1D **13**
Westoning. *Beds* —3B **28**
Weston Longville. *Norf*
—1A **18**
Weston Turville. *Buck*
—2A **36**
Weston Underwood. *Buck*
—1A **28**
West Perry. *Camb* —3C **21**
West Poringland. *Norf*
—2B **18**
West Raynham. *Norf* —3B **8**
West Row. *Suff* —2D **23**
West Rudham. *Norf* —3B **8**
West Runton. *Norf* —1A **10**
Westry. *Camb* —3A **14**
West Somerton. *Norf* —1D **19**
West Stow. *Suff* —2B **24**
West Tofts. *Norf* —3B **16**
West Walton. *Norf* —1B **14**
Westwick. *Camb* —3B **22**
Westwick. *Norf* —3B **10**
West Wickham. *Camb*
—2D **31**
West Willoughby. *Linc* —1A **4**
West Winch. *Norf* —1D **15**
Westwood. *Camb* —3C **13**
West Wratting. *Camb*
—1D **31**
Wetherden. *Suff* —3D **25**
Wetheringsett. *Suff* —3A **26**
Wethersfield. *Essx* —3A **32**
Wetherup Street. *Suff*
—3A **26**
Weybourne. *Norf* —1A **10**
Weybread. *Suff* —1B **26**
Whaddon. *Camb* —2A **30**
Whaplode. *Linc* —3A **6**
Whaplode Drove. *Linc*
—1A **14**
Whaplode St Catherine. *Linc*
—3A **6**

Wharley End. *Beds* —2A **28**
Whatfield. *Suff* —2D **33**
Wheatacre. *Norf* —3D **19**
Wheathampstead. *Hert*
—2C **37**
Whelpley Hill. *Buck* —3A **36**
Whepstead. *Suff* —1B **32**
Wherstead. *Suff* —2A **34**
Whimpwell Green. *Norf*
—3C **11**
Whinburgh. *Norf* —2D **17**
Whipsnade. *Beds* —2B **36**
Whissonsett. *Norf* —3C **9**
Whiston. *Nptn* —3A **20**
Whiteash Green. *Essx* —3A **32**
White Colne. *Essx* —1B **40**
White Horse Common. *Norf*
—3C **11**
White Notley. *Essx* —2A **40**
White Roding. *Essx* —2C **39**
Whitestreet Green. *Suff*
—3C **33**
Whitington. *Norf* —3A **16**
Whittlesey. *Camb* —3D **13**
Whittlesford. *Camb* —2B **30**
Whitwell. *Hert* —1C **37**
Whitwell. *Leic* —2A **12**
Wicken. *Camb* —2C **23**
Wicken Bonhunt. *Essx*
—3B **30**
Wicker Street Green. *Suff*
—2C **33**
Wickham Bishops. *Essx*
—2B **40**
Wickhambrook. *Suff* —1A **32**
Wickham Green. *Suff* —3D **25**
Wickham Market. *Suff*
—1B **34**
Wickhampton. *Norf* —2D **19**
Wickham St Paul. *Essx*
—3B **32**
Wickham Skeith. *Suff*
—3D **25**
Wickham Street. *Suff* —3D **25**
Wicklewood. *Norf* —2D **17**
Wickmere. *Norf* —2A **10**
Widdington. *Essx* —3C **31**
Widford. *Essx* —3D **39**
Widford. *Hert* —2B **38**
Wiggenhall St Germans. *Norf*
—1C **15**
Wiggenhall St Mary Magdalen.
Norf —1C **15**
Wiggenhall St Mary the Virgin.
Norf —1C **15**
Wiggenhall St Peter. *Norf*
—1D **15**
Wiggens Green. *Essx* —2D **31**
Wigginton. *Hert* —2A **36**
Wighton. *Norf* —1C **9**
Wigsthorpe. *Nptn* —1B **20**
Wigtoft. *Linc* —2D **5**
Wilburton. *Camb* —2B **22**
Wilby. *Norf* —1D **25**
Wilby. *Nptn* —3A **20**
Wilby. *Suff* —2B **26**
Wilden. *Beds* —1B **28**
Wilde Street. *Suff* —2A **24**
Willen. *Buck* —2A **28**
Willian. *Hert* —3D **29**
Willingale. *Essx* —3C **39**
Willingham. *Camb* —2B **22**
Willingham Green. *Camb*
—1D **31**
Willington. *Beds* —2C **29**
Willisham Tye. *Suff* —1D **33**
Willows Green. *Essx* —2A **40**

Wilney Green. *Norf* —1D **25**
Wilsford. *Linc* —1B **4**
Wilstead. *Beds* —2B **28**
Wilsthorpe. *Linc* —1B **12**
Wilstone. *Hert* —2A **36**
Wimbish. *Essx* —3C **31**
Wimbish Green. *Essx* —3D **31**
Wimblington. *Camb* —3B **14**
Wimbotsham. *Norf* —2D **15**
Windsor Green. *Suff* —1B **32**
Winfarthing. *Norf* —1A **26**
Wing. *Buck* —1A **36**
Wing. *Leic* —2A **12**
Wingfield. *Beds* —1B **36**
Wingfield. *Suff* —2B **26**
Wingrave. *Buck* —2A **36**
Winston. *Suff* —3A **26**
Winterton-on-Sea. *Norf*
—1D **19**
Winwick. *Camb* —1C **21**
Wisbech. *Camb* —1B **14**
Wisbech St Mary. *Camb*
—2B **14**
Wissett. *Suff* —2C **27**
Wistow. *Camb* —1D **21**
Witcham. *Camb* —1B **22**
Witchford. *Camb* —2C **23**
Witham. *Essx* —2B **40**
Witham on the Hill. *Linc*
—1B **12**
Withergate. *Norf* —3B **10**
Withermarsh Green. *Suff*
—3D **33**
Withersdale Street. *Suff*
—1B **26**
Withersfield. *Suff* —2D **31**
Witnesham. *Suff* —1A **34**
Wittering. *Camb* —2B **12**
Witton. *Norf* —2C **19**
Witton Bridge. *Norf* —2C **11**
Wivenhoe. *Essx* —1D **41**
Wiveton. *Norf* —1D **9**
Wix. *Essx* —1A **42**
Wixoe. *Suff* —2A **32**
Woburn. *Beds* —3A **28**
Woburn Sands. *Buck* —3A **28**
Wolferton. *Norf* —3D **7**
Wollaston. *Nptn* —3A **20**
Wolterton. *Norf* —2A **10**
Woodbastwick. *Norf* —1C **19**
Woodbridge. *Suff* —2B **34**
Wood Dalling. *Norf* —3D **9**
Woodditton. *Camb* —1D **31**
Wood End. *Hert* —1A **38**
Woodend Green. *Essx*
—1C **39**
Woodford. *Nptn* —2A **20**
Woodgate. *Norf* —1D **17**
Woodham Ferrers. *Essx*
—3A **40**
Woodham Mortimer. *Essx*
—3B **40**
Woodham Walter. *Essx*
—3B **40**
Woodhurst. *Camb* —2A **22**
Woodnewton. *Nptn* —3B **12**
Woodnook. *Linc* —2A **4**
Wood Norton. *Norf* —3D **9**
Woodrising. *Norf* —2C **17**
Woodside. *Hert* —3D **37**
Woodston. *Camb* —3C **13**
Woodton. *Norf* —3B **18**
Woodwalton. *Camb* —1D **21**
Woolley. *Camb* —2C **21**
Woolmer Green. *Hert* —2D **37**
Woolpit. *Suff* —3C **25**
Woolsthorpe. *Linc* —3A **4**

❑ Opening times for Places of Interest vary greatly; while some open all year, others open only for the summer season, some only open certain days or even part days.   We recommend, to avoid disappointment, you check with the nearest Tourist Information Centre (see below) before starting your journey.

❑ This is an index to selected features shown on the map pages, it is not a comprehensive guide.

❑ To keep the maps as clear as possible, descriptive words like 'Castle', 'Museum' etc. are omitted, a key to the various map symbols used can be found on page 1 in the reference.   Features within very congested areas and town centres are indicated as space allows, wherever possible, at least with the appropriate symbol; in some instances the text may fall into an adjacent map square.

❑ Every possible care has been taken to ensure that the information given is accurate and whilst the publishers would be grateful to learn of any errors, they regret they cannot accept any responsibility for loss thereby caused.

Abbey/Friary/Priory

Beeston Priory, Beeston Regis
    —1A 10
Binham Priory—1C 9
Burnham Norton Friary,
    Burnham Market—1B 8
Bury St Edmunds Abbey—3B 24
Bushmead Priory—3C 21
Castle Acre Priory—1B 16
Clare Priory—2A 32
Creake Abbey, North Creake
    —2B 8
Denny Abbey, Denny End—3B 22
Dunwich Greyfriars—2D 27
Greyfriars' Cloisters, Great
    Yarmouth—2D 19
Greyfriars Tower, King's Lynn
    —1D 15
Leiston Abbey—3D 27
Ramsey Abbey—1D 21
Royston Priory & St John the
    Baptist Church—2A 30
St Benet's Abbey, Johnson's
    Street—1C 19
St Botolph's Priory, Colchester
    —1D 41
St Faith's Priory, Horsham St
    Faith—1B 18
St Leonard's Priory, Stamford
    —2B 12
St Olaves Priory—3D 19
St Osyth Priory—2A 42
Thetford Priory—1B 24
Walsingham Abbey & Priory, Little
    Walsingham—2C 9
Ware Priory—2A 38
Weybourne Priory—1A 10

Wymondham Abbey & Church
    —2A 18

Aquarium

Great Yarmouth Sea Life
    Centre—2D 19
Hunstanton Sea Life Centre
    —1D 7
Mickfield Fish & Water Garden
    —3A 26
Waveney Fish Farm, Diss—2A 26

Arboretum

See also Garden

Barnsdale Arboretum, Whitwell
    —2A 12
Blakenham Woodland Garden,
    Little Blakenham—2A 34
Lynford Arboretum, Mundford
    —3B 16
Whipsnade Tree Cathedral
    —2B 36

Bird Garden

See also Farm Park, Wildlife Park, Zoo

Kelly's Birds & Aviaries, Kelling
    —1D 9
Peakirk Wildfowl Gardens—2C 13
Stagsden Bird Gardens—2A 28
Pensthorpe Waterfowl Park,
    Falkenham—3C 9

Botanical Garden

Cambridge University Botanic
    Garden—1B 30

Spalding Tropical Forest,
    Pinchbeck—3D 5

Broads Authority Information Centres

*See also Tourist Information
Centres   NOTE: Telephone
Numbers are given in Italics*

Beccles—3D 19   *01502 713196*
Hoveton—1C 19   *01603 782281*
Ranworth—1C 19   *01603 270453*
Toad Hole Cottage, How Hill
    —1C 19   *01692 678763*

Butterfly Farm

Barrow Tropical Butterfly
    Garden—3A 24
Great Yarmouth Living Jungle &
    Butterfly Farm—2D 19
Hopton Butterfly & Bird World,
    Hopton on Sea—3D 19
Long Sutton Butterfly & Falconry
    Park, Little London—3B 6
Rutland Water Butterfly & Aquatic
    Centre, Empingham—2A 12

Castle and Garden

See also Castle
Rockingham Castle—3A 12

Castle

See also Castle & Garden

Anstey Castle—3B 30
Baconsthorpe Castle—2A 10
Bedford Castle—2B 28
Benington Castle—1D 37
Berkhamsted Castle—3A 36

Bourne Castle—1B 12
Bungay Castle—1C 27
Burwell Castle—3C 23
Caister Castle, West Caister
    —1D 19
Cambridge Castle—1B 30
Castle Acre Castle—1B 16
Castle Rising Castle—3D 7
Clare Castle—2A 32
Colchester Castle—1C 41
Eaton Socon Castle—1C 29
Ely Castle—2C 23
Eye Castle—2A 26
Fotheringhay Castle—3B 12
Framlingham Castle—3B 26
Haughley Castle—3D 25
Hedingham Castle, Castle
    Hedingham—3A 32
Hertford Castle—2A 38
Horsford Castle—1B 18
Huntingdon Castle—2D 21
Lavendon Castle—1A 28
Lidgate Castle—1A 32
New Buckenham Castle—3D 17
Norwich Castle—2B 18
Oakham Castle—2A 12
Ongar Castle, Chipping Ongar
    —3C 39
Orford Castle—2D 35
Pleshey Castle—2D 39
Saffron Walden Castle—3C 31
Someries Castle, Chiltern
    Green—2C 37
Stansted Mountfitchet Castle
    —1C 39
Swineshead Castle, Baythorpe
    —1D 5
Thetford Castle—1B 24
Totternhoe Castle—1A 36
Weeting Castle—1A 24
Weston Turville Castle—2A 36
Woodwalton Castle, Church
    End—1D 21

Scott's Grotto, Ware—2A 38

Country Park

Barnwell Country Park, Oundle
    —1B 20
Brandon Country Park—1A 24
Brigstock Country Park—1A 20
Clare Castle Country Park—2A 32
Cudmore Grove Country Park,
    East Mersea—2D 41
Danbury Country Park—3A 40
Dunstable Downs Country Park
    —2B 36
Easton Farm Park—1B 34
Emberton Country Park—1A 28
Ferry Meadows Country Park,
    Peterborough—3C 13
Fritton Lake Country Park—2D 19
Great Cornard Country Park
    —3B 32
Harrold-Odell Country Park
    —1A 28
Hatfield Forest Country Park,
    Takeley Street—2C 39
High Woods Country Park, Mile
    End—1D 41
Hinchingbrooke Country Park,
    Huntingdon—2D 21
Holland Haven Country Park,
    Holland-on-Sea—2B 42
Holt Woodlands Country Park
    —2D 9
Irchester Country Park—3A 20
Knettishall Heath Country Park,
    Rushford—1C 25
Lee Valley Park, Waltham
    Cross—3A 38
Lonely Farm Leisure Park,
    Saxmundham—3C 27
Marsh Farm Country Park, South
    Woodham Ferrers—3B 40
Northaw Great Wood Country
    Park—3D 37
Priory Country Park, Bedford
    —2B 28
Rutland Water Country Park
    —2A 12
Sandringham Country Park—3D 7
Stewartby Lake Country Park
    —2B 28
Stockgrove Country Park, Great
    Brickhill—1A 36
Sundon Hills Country Park, Upper
    Sundon—1B 36
Trent Park Country Park,
    Cockfosters—3D 37
Wandlebury Country Park,
    Cambridge—1B 30

West Stow Country Park—2A 24

Farm Park/Working Farm

See also Wildlife Park

Bowmans Open Farm, London
    Colney—3C 37
Bury Farm Centre, Epping—3B 38
Cranes Watering Farm,
    Harleston—1B 26
Dedham Rare Breeds Farm
    —3D 33
Gray's Honey Farm, Chatteris
    —1A 22
Hayes Hill Farm, Holyfield—3A 38
Marsh Farm, South Woodham
    Ferrers—3B 40
Oak Farm Rare Breeds Park,
    Aylesbury—2A 36
Park Farm, Snettisham—2D 7
Rutland Farm Park, Oakham
    —2A 12
Stags Holt Farm Park,
    Chainbridge—2B 14
Standalone Farm Centre,
    Letchworth—3D 29
Teddy's Farm, Beckingham—1A 4
Union Farm, Gressenhall—1C 17
Water Hall Farm & Craft Centre,
    Whitwell—1C 37

Fortress

Felixstowe 'Q' Tower—3B 34
Harwich Redoubt—3B 34
Landguard Fort, Felixstowe
    —3B 34
Martello Tower No. 1, Point
    Clear—2D 41

Garden

*See also Historic Building &
Garden*

Akenfield Garden, Charsfield
    —1B 34
Alby Gardens, Erpingham—2B 10
Barnsdale Drought Garden,
    Whitwell—2A 12
BBC Essex Garden, Abridge
    —3B 38
Benington Lordship Gardens
    —1D 37
Beth Chatto Gardens, Elmstead
    Market—1D 41
Blake Hall Gardens,
    Bobbingworth—3C 39
Bressingham Dell Garden—1D 25
Bridge End Gardens, Saffron
    Walden—3C 31

Bruisyard Herb & Water
Gardens—3C 27
Byways Water Gardens, Soham
—2C 23
Capel Manor Gardens, Crews
Hill—3A 38
Castle Ashby Gardens—1A 28
Cheslyn Gardens, Watford
—3C 37
Congham Hall Herb Gardens,
Grimston—3A 8
Craft at the Suffolk Barn Gardens,
Great Barton—3B 24
Crossing House Garden,
Shepreth—2A 30
Docwra's Manor Gardens,
Shepreth—2A 30
East Bergholt Lodge Gardens
—3D 33
Fairhaven Garden Trust, South
Walsham—1C 19
Feeringbury Manor Garden
Feering—1B 40
Gardens of The Rose, Chiswell
Green—3C 37
Gifford's Hall Gardens, Hartest
,—1B 32
Glavenside Gardens,
Letheringsett—2D 9
Gooderstone Water Gardens
—2A 16
Harlaxton Manor Gardens—2A 4
Helmingham Hall Gardens
—1A 34
Hill Farm Herbs, Brigstock—1A 20
Hoveton Hall Gardens,
Wroxham—3C 11
Hyde Hall Gardens, Woodham
Ferrers—3A 40
Hylands Park Gardens,
Chelmsford—3D 39
Le Grice Garden Centre Rose
Fields, North Walsham—3B 10
Mannington Hall Gardens,
Saxthorpe—2A 10
Mark Hall Gardens, Harlow
—2B 38
Millennium Garden, Maldon
—3B 40
Natural Surroundings Gardens,
Glandford—1D 9
Norfolk Lavender, Heacham
—2D 7
Paradise Centre Gardens,
Lamarsh—3B 32
Poplar Lane Thompson & Morgan
Trial Gardens, Chantry—2A 34
Rainthorpe Hall Gardens,
Tasburgh—3B 18

Raveningham Hall Gardens
—3C 19
Royston Priory Gardens—2A 30
St Osyth Priory Gardens—2A 42
Saling Hall Garden, Great
Saling—1A 40
Spains Hall Garden,
Finchingfield—3D 31
Springfields Gardens, Spalding
—3D 5
Stockwood Gardens, Luton
—2B 36
Swiss Garden, Ickwell—2C 29
Thornham Herb Walled Garden,
Thornham Magna—2A 26
Venns Farm Garden, Middlewood
Green—3A 26
Ware Priory Gardens—2A 38
Wilburton Herb Garden—2B 22
Wolterton Hall Gardens—2A 10

Hill Figure

See also Prehistoric Monument

Whipsnade White Lion—2A 36

Hill Fort

Beacon Hill Hill Fort, Ivinghoe
—2A 36
Cholesbury Camp Hill Fort
—3A 36
Sandy Caesar's Camp—2C 29
Wandlebury Hill Fort,
Cambridge—1C 31
Warham St Mary Hill Fort—1C 9

Historic Building & Garden

See also Historic Building

Anglesey Abbey, Lode—3C 23
Ascott, Wing—1A 36
Beeston Hall, Neatishead—3C 11
Belton House, Grantham—2A 4
Blickling Hall—3A 10
Chenies Manor House—3B 36
Deene Park—3A 12
Elton Hall—3B 12
Euston Hall—2B 24
Felbrigg Hall—2A 10
Fulbeck Hall—1A 4
Grimsthorpe Castle—3B 4
Haughley Park, Wetherden
—3D 25
Holkham Hall—1B 8
Ickworth, Horringer—3B 24
Ingatestone Hall—3D 39
Kentwell Hall, Long Melford
—2B 32

Kirby Hall, Corby—3A 12
Knebworth House, Old
Knebworth—1D 37
Layer Marney Tower—2C 41
Luton Hoo—2C 37
Melford Hall, Long Melford
—2B 32
Otley Hall—1B 34
Oxburgh Hall, Oxborough—2A 16
Peckover House, Wisbech
—2B 14
Pleasaunce, The, Overstrand
—1B 10
Priory, The, Lavenham—2C 33
Sandringham House—3D 7
Somerleyton Hall—3D 19
Wimpole Hall, Arrington—1A 30
Wingfield College—2B 26
Wrest Park House, Silsoe—3B 28

Historic Building

*See also Historic Building &
Garden*

Audley End House—3C 31
Blakeney Guildhall—1D 9
Boughton House, Geddington
—1A 20
Browne's Hospital, Stamford
—2B 12
Buckden Palace—3C 21
Burghley House, Stamford
—2B 12
Bury St Edmunds Theatre
Royal—3B 24
Chichele College, Higham
Ferrers—3A 20
Chicheley Hall—2A 28
Chicksands Priory, Shefford
—3C 29
Christchurch Mansion, Ipswich
—2A 34
Coggeshall Grange Barn—1B 40
Cressing Temple Barn,
Cressing—2A 40
Dragon Hall, Norwich—2B 18
Fen Cottage, Wicken—2C 23
Flatford Bridge Cottage, East
Bergholt—3D 33
Forty Hall, Enfield—3A 38
Fydell House, Boston—1A 6
Gorhambury, St Albans—3C 37
Gosfield Hall—1A 40
Hadleigh Guildhall—2D 33
Hatfield House—3D 37
Hinchingbrooke House,
Huntingdon—2D 21
Houghton Hall, New Houghton
—3A 8

Houghton House, Ampthill—3B 28
Island Hall, Godmanchester
    —2D 21
Kimbolton Castle—3B 20
King's Lynn St George's
    Guildhall—3D 7
Little Hall, Lavenham—2C 33
Longthorpe Tower,
    Peterborough—3C 13
Lyddington Bede House—3A 12
Lyveden New Bield, Brigstock
    —1A 20
Mentmore Towers—2A 36
Nether Hall, Cavendish—2B 32
New Inn, Peasenhall—3C 27
Old Gorhambury House, St
    Albans—3C 37
Old Merchant's House, Great
    Yarmouth—2D 19
Oliver Cromwell's House, Ely
    —1C 23
Paycocke's, Coggeshall—1B 40
Prebendal Manor House, The,
    Nassington—3B 12
Priors Hall Barn, Widdington
    —3C 31
Ramsey Abbey Gatehouse
    —1D 21
Row 111 Houses, Great
    Yarmouth—2D 19
Rye House Gatehouse,
    Hoddesdon—3A 38
St Albans Clocktower—3C 37
St Giles Leper Hospital, Maldon
    —3B 40
St John's Abbey Gate,
    Colchester—1C 41
Shalom Hall, Layer Breton
    —2C 41
Shaw's Corner, Ayot St
    Lawrence—2C 37
Southwick Hall—3B 12
Thaxted Guildhall—3D 31
Thetford Warren Lodge—1B 24
Trinity Hospital, Castle Rising
    —3D 7
True's Yard Fishermen's
    Cottages, King's Lynn—3D 7
Waltham Abbey Gatehouse
    —3A 38
Woburn Abbey—3A 28
Woolsthorpe Manor—3A 4

Fakenham Racecourse—3C 9
Great Yarmouth Racecourse
    —1D 19

Huntingdon Racecourse,
    Brampton—2D 21
Newmarket Racecourse—3D 23

See also Windmill

Bourne Mill, Colchester—1D 41
Bromham Mill, Bridge End—1B 28
Cogglesford Watermill, Sleaford
    —1B 4
Easterford Watermill, Kelvedon
    —2B 40
Ford End Watermill, Ivinghoe
    —2A 36
Gunton Park Sawmill, Suffield
    —2B 10
Hinxton Watermill—2B 30
Houghton Watermill—2D 21
Kingsbury Watermill, St Albans
    —3C 37
Letheringham Watermill—1B 34
Letheringsett Watermill—2D 9
Little Welnetham Rake Factory,
    Bradfield St Clare—1B 32
Lode Watermill—3C 23
Mill Green Museum & Mill,
    Hatfield—3D 37
Pakenham Watermill, Grimstone
    End—3C 25
Pinchbeck Engine—3D 5
Sacrewell Watermill,
    Thornhaugh—2B 12
Snettisham Watermill,
    Southgate—2D 7
Stretham Beam Engine—2C 23
Thorrington Tide Mill—2D 41
Woodbridge Tide Mill—2B 34

Happisburgh Lighthouse—2C 11
Harwich Low Lighthouse—3B 34

Santa Pod Raceway—3A 20
Snetterton Motor Circuit—1D 25

100th Bomb Group Memorial Air
    Museum, Thorpe Abbotts
    —1A 26
Alby Bottle Museum,
    Erpingham—2B 10
Alby Lace Museum, Erpingham
    —2B 10
Aldeburgh Moot Hall—1D 35
Amersham Museum—3A 36

Ashton Mill Museum—1B 20
Ayscoughfee Hall, Spalding
    —3D 5
Bardfield Cottage Museum, Great
    Bardfield—3D 31
Beccles & District Museum
    Beccles—3D 19
Bedford Museum—2B 28
Bishop Bonner's Cottage,
    Dereham—1C 17
Blake Hall War Museum,
    Bobbingworth—3C 39
Boston Guildhall Museum—1A 6
Braintree District Museum—1A 40
Braintree Town Hall Centre
    —1A 40
Brandon Heritage Centre—1A 24
Bressingham Steam Museum
    —1D 25
Bridewell Museum, Norwich
    —2B 18
Brightlingsea Museum—2D 41
Broads Museum, Sutton—3C 11
Bungay Museum—1C 27
Bunyan Meeting Library &
    Museum, Bedford—2B 28
Burnham-on-Crouch & District
    Museums—3C 41
Burston Strike School Museum
    —1A 26
Bury St Edmunds Art Gallery
    —3B 24
Bury St Edmunds Clock
    Museum—3B 24
Bygones at Holkham—1B 8
Caister Castle Motor Museum,
    West Caister—1D 19
Cambridge & County Folk
    Museum—1B 30
Cambridge Darkroom—1B 30
Cambridge Museum of
    Technology—1B 30
Cambridge University Museum of
    Archaeology & Anthropology
    —1B 30
Cambridge University Museum of
    Classical Archaeology—1B 30
Cambridge University Museum of
    Mineralogy & Petrology—1B 30
Cambridge University Museum of
    Zoology—1B 30
Cecil Higgins Art Gallery &
    Museum, Bedford—2B 28
Charles Burrell Museum,
    Thetford—1B 24
Chatteris Museum—1A 22
Chelmsford & Essex Museum
    Chelmsford—3A 40
City of Norwich Aviation Museum,

Horsham St Faith—1B 18

Clare Ancient House Museum
—2A 32

Cockthorpe Hall Toy Museum
—1C 9

Coggeshall Heritage Museum
—1B 40

Colchester Natural History
Museum—1C 41

Colchester Social History
Museum—1C 41

Colman's Mustard Museum,
Norwich—2B 18

Colne Valley Railway Museum,
Castle Hedingham—3A 32

Cotton Mechanical Music
Museum—3D 25

Cowper & Newton Museum,
Olney—1A 28

Cranwell Aviation Heritage
Centre, North Rauceby—1B 4

Cromer Lifeboat Museum—1B 10

Cromer Museum—1B 10

Cromwell Museum, Huntingdon
—2D 21

Dedham Toy Museum—3D 33

Diss Museum—2A 26

Dorothy L. Sayers Centre,
Witham—2B 40

Dunham Museum, Little
Dunham—1B 16

Dunwich Museum—2D 27

Dunwich Underwater Exploration
Exhibition, Orford—1D 35

Duxford Imperial War Museum
—2B 30

East Anglian Life, Museum of,
Stowmarket—1D 33

East Anglian Railway Museum,
Wakes Colne—1B 40

East Anglia Transport Museum,
Carlton Colville—3D 19

East Essex Aviation & Forties
Museum, Point Clear—2D 41

Easton Farm Park Vintage Farm
Machinery Collection—1B 34

Elizabethan House Museum,
Great Yarmouth—2D 19

Elstow Moot Hall—2B 28

Ely Museum—1C 23

Ely Stained Glass Museum
—1C 23

Entertainment, Museum of,
Whaplode St Catherine—1A 14

Epping Forest District Museum,
Waltham Cross—3A 38

Evergreen Christmas World,
Upwell—2B 14

Fakenham Museum of Gas &

Local History—3C 9

Feering & Kelvedon Local History
Museum, Kelvedon—2B 40

Fenland Aviation Museum,
Wisbech—1B 14

Finchingfield Guildhall Museum
—3D 31

First Garden City Heritage
Museum, Letchworth—3D 29

Fitzwilliam Museum, Cambridge
—1B 30

Flag Fen Bronze Age
Excavations, Peterborough
—3D 13

Flatford Granary Bygones
Collection, East Bergholt
—3D 33

Forncett Industrial Steam
Museum, Forncett St Mary
—3A 18

Forty Hall Museum, Enfield
—3A 38

Fry Art Gallery, The, Saffron
Walden—3C 31

Gainsborough's House Museum,
Sudbury—2B 32

Glandford Shell Museum—1D 9

Gordon Boswell Romany
Museum, Clay Lake—3D 5

Grantham Museum—2A 4

Great Yarmouth Museums'
Exhibition Galleries—2D 19

Haddenham Farmland Museum
—2B 22

Halesworth Art Gallery—2C 27

Halesworth & District Museum
—2C 27

Harlow Museum—3B 38

Harwich Maritime Museum
—3B 34

Haverhill & District Local History
Museum—2D 31

Hertford Museum—2A 38

Hollytrees Museum, Colchester
—1C 41

House on the Hill Toy Museum,
Stansted Mountfitchet—1C 39

Iceni Village & Museums, Cockley
Cley—2A 16

Ipswich Museum & Exhibition
Gallery—2A 34

Irchester Narrow Gauge Railway
Museum—3A 20

Kettering Manor House
Museum—2A 20

Kettle's Yard, Cambridge—1B 30

King's Lynn Centre Art Gallery
—3D 7

King's Lynn Old Gaol House

Museum & Regalia Rooms
—1D 15

Landguard Fort Museum,
Felixstowe—3B 34

Lanman Museum, Framlingham
—3B 26

Lavenham Guildhall—2C 33

Laxfield & District Museum
—2B 26

Letchworth Museum—3D 29

Longsands Museum, St Neots
—3C 21

Long Shop Museum, Leiston
—3D 27

Lowestoft & East Suffolk Maritime
Museum—3D 19

Lowestoft Museum—3D 19

Lowewood Museum,
Broxbourne—3A 38

Luton Museum & Art Gallery
—1B 36

Lynn Museum, King's Lynn—3D 7

Maldon Museum—3B 40

Manningtree Museum, Mistley
—3A 34

March & District Museum—3B 14

Maritime Museum of East Anglia,
Great Yarmouth—2D 19

Mark Hall Cycle Museum,
Harlow—2B 38

Mersea Island Museum, West
Mersea—2D 41

Mid-Suffolk Light Railway,
Wetheringsett—3A 26

Mildenhall & District Museum
—2A 24

Milton Keynes Exhibition
Gallery—3A 28

Mosquito Aircraft Museum,
London Colney—3C 37

Moyse's Hall Museum, Bury St
Edmunds—3B 24

Much Hadham Forge Museum
—2B 38

Muckleborough Military Museum,
Weybourne—1D 9

National Horse Racing Museum,
Newmarket—3D 23

Nene Valley Railway Museum,
Stibbington—3B 12

Norfolk Rural Life Museum,
Gressenhall—1C 17

Norfolk & Suffolk Aviation
Museum, Flixton—1C 27

Normanton Church Museum,
Edith Weston—2A 12

Norris Museum, St Ives—2A 22

North Creake Forge Museum
—2B 8

North Ings Farm Museum, Dorrington—1B 4
North Norfolk Railway Museum, Sheringham—1A 10
North Weald Airfield Memorial Museum, North Weald Bassett—3B 38
Norwich Castle Museum—2B 18
Norwich St Peter Hungate Church Museum—2B 18
Parham 390th Bomb Group Memorial Air Museum—3C 27
Peterborough City Museum & Art Gallery—3C 13
Pitstone Green Farm Museum —2A 36
Prickwillow Engine Museum —1C 23
Ramsey Rural Museum—1D 21
Rebel Air Museum, Earls Colne —1B 40
Rhodes Memorial Museum & Commonwealth Centre, Bishop's Stortford—1B 38
Royal Naval Patrol Service Museum, Lowestoft—3D 19
Royal Norfolk Regimental Museum, Norwich—2B 18
Royston & District Museum —2A 30
Rushden Historical Transport Museum—3A 20
Rutland County Museum, Oakham—2A 12
Rutland Railway Museum, Cottesmore—1A 12
Sacrewell Farm & Country Centre, Thornhaugh—2B 12
Saffron Walden Museum—3C 31
Sainsbury Centre for Visual Arts, Colney—2A 18
St Albans Museum—3C 37
St Albans Organ Museum—3C 37
Scott Polar Research Institute, Cambridge—1B 30
Sedgwick Museum of Geology, Cambridge—1B 30
Shirehall Museum, Little Walsingham—2C 9
Shuttleworth Collection, Old Warden—2C 29
Sir Alfred Munnings Art Museum, Dedham Heath—3D 33
Southwold Lifeboat Museum —2D 27
Southwold Museum—2D 27
Southwold Sailors Reading Room—2D 27
Stamford Museum—2B 12

Stamford Steam Brewery Museum—2B 12
Station 146, Seething Airfield Control Tower Museum—3C 19
Stevenage Museum—1D 37
Stockwood Craft Museum, Luton—2B 36
Stonehenge Works Railway Museum, Leighton Buzzard —1A 36
Strangers' Hall Museum of Domestic Life, Norwich—2B 18
Strumpshaw Hall Steam Museum—2C 19
Sue Ryder Foundation Museum, Cavendish—2B 32
Suffolk Regimental Museum, Bury St Edmunds—3B 24
Swaffham Museum—2B 16
Thetford Ancient House Museum—1B 24
Thorney Heritage Centre—2D 13
Thorpeness Windmill Museum —1D 35
Thursford Collection, Thursford Green—2C 9
Toad Hole Cottage Marshmans Museum, How Hill—1C 19
Tolhouse Museum, Great Yarmouth—2D 19
Town House Museum of Lynn Life, King's Lynn—1D 15
Verulamium Museum, St Albans—3C 37
Walsham-le-Willows Local History Museum—2D 25
Walter Rothschild Zoological Museum, Tring—2A 36
Walton Maritime Museum, Walton-on-the-Naze—1B 42
Ware Museum—2A 38
Wartime Watton Museum—2C 17
Watford Museum—3C 37
Wellingborough Heritage Centre—3A 20
Whipple Museum of the History of Science, Cambridge—1B 30
Whittlesey Museum—3D 13
William Clowes Print Museum, Beccles—1D 27
Willoughby Memorial Trust Gallery, Corby Glen—3A 4
Wimpole Home Farm, Arrington —1A 30
Wisbech & Fenland Museum Wisbech—2B 14
Witham Fossil Hall, Silver End —2B 40
Woburn Heritage Centre—3A 28

Wolferton Station Museum—3D 7
Wollaston Museum—3A 20
Wolsey Art Gallery, Ipswich —2A 34
Woodbridge Museum—2B 34
Woolpit Bygones Room—3C 25
Working Silk Museum, The, Braintree—1A 40
Wymondham Heritage Museum —2A 18

Nature Reserve/Bird Sanctuary

R.S.P.B., English Nature & Wildfowl Trust

Barnack Hills & Holes Nature Reserve—2B 12
Barton Hills Nature Reserve, Barton-le-Clay—1B 36
Benacre Broad Bird Sanctuary, Covehithe—1D 27
Berney Marshes Bird Sanctuary, Halvergate Marshes—2D 19
Blakeney Point Bird Sanctuary —1D 9
Brancaster Marshes Nature Reserve—1A 8
Breydon Water Bird Sanctuary, Great Yarmouth—2D 19
Castor Hanglands Nature Reserve, Upton—2C 13
Cavenham Heath Nature Reserve, Icklingham—2A 24
Chippenham Fen Nature Reserve—3D 23
Cockshoot Broad Nature Reserve, Woodbastwick—1C 19
Dengie Marshes Nature Reserve, Tillingham—3D 41
Dunwich Heath Nature Reserve —3D 27
Fowlmere Bird Sanctuary—2B 30
Frampton Marshes Bird Sanctuary—2A 6
Hamford Water Bird Sanctuary, Walton-on-the-Naze—1B 42
Havergate Island Bird Sanctuary, Orford—2D 35
Hickling Broad Nature Reserve —3D 11
Holkham Nature Reserve—1B 8
Horsey Mere Bird Sanctuary —3D 11
Lodge Bird Sanctuary, The, Sandy—2C 29
Minsmere Bird Sanctuary, Westleton—3D 27
Morston Marshes Bird Sanctuary—1D 9

Nene Washes Bird Sanctuary,
Whittlesey—3D 13
North Warren Bird Sanctuary,
Aldringham—1D 35
Old Hall Marshes Bird Sanctuary,
Tollesbury—2C 41
Orfordness Bird Sanctuary
—2D 35
Ouse Washes Bird Sanctuary,
Welches Dam—1B 22
Ranworth Broad Nature
Reserve—1C 19
Rockland Marshes Nature
Reserve, Rockland St Mary
—2C 19
Rye House Marsh Bird Sanctuary,
Hoddesdon—2A 38
Scolt Head Island Nature
Reserve—1B 8
Snettisham Bird Sanctuary,
Shepherd's Port—2D 7
Stiffkey Marshes Bird Sanctuary
—1C 9
Stour Wood & Copperas Bay
Nature Reserve, Wrabness
—3A 34
Strumpshaw Fen Bird
Sanctuary—2C 19
Surlingham (Church) Marshes
Nature Reserve—2C 19
Titchwell Marsh Bird Sanctuary
—1A 8
Tringford Reservoirs Bird
Sanctuary, Marsworth—2A 36
Walberswick Bird Sanctuary
—2D 27
Weeting Heath Nature Reserve
—1A 24
Welney Wildfowl Refuge—3C 15
Westleton Heath Nature
Reserve—3D 27
Wicken Fen Nature Reserve
—2C 23
Wilstone Reservoir Bird
Sanctuary—2A 36
Winterton Dunes Nature Reserve,
Winterton-on-Sea—3D 11
Wolves Wood Nature Reserve,
Hadleigh—2D 33

Ada Cole Memorial Stables,
Broadley Common—3B 38
African Violet Centre, Terrington
St Clement—1C 15
Anglian Water Birdwatching
Centre, Egleton—2A 12
Ashridge Estate, Ringshall

—2A 36
Baldock's Mill Heritage Centre,
Bourne—1B 12
Bardfield Cage, Great Bardfield
—3D 31
Baytree Owl Centre, Weston
—3D 5
Bellmount Tower, Grantham
—2A 4
Bexwell Hall Dried Flower
Centre—2D 15
Binham Wayside Cross—2C 9
Blakeney Point Information
Centre—1D 9
Blakeney Point/ Morston Marshes/
Stiffkey Marshes—1C 9
Blickling Mausoleum—3A 10
Boatworld, Lowestoft—3D 19
Boston St Botolph's Church
(Boston Stump)—1A 6
Bradwell Power Station Visitor
Centre, Bradwell Waterside
—3D 41
Brancaster Marshes/ Scolt Head
Island—1A 8
Bridge Cottage Information
Centre, East Bergholt—3D 33
Broadland Conservation Centre,
Ranworth—1C 19
Caithness Crystal Visitor Centre,
King's Lynn—1D 15
Cambridge Brass Rubbing
Centre—1B 30
Cambridge Holy Sepulchre Round
Church—1B 30
Castle Acre Bailey Gate—1B 16
Caxton Gibbet—3D 21
Chiltern Brewery, Terrick—3A 36
Cider Place, The, Ilketshall St
Lawrence—1C 27
Clipsham Yew Tree Avenue
—1A 12
Covehithe Church Ruins—1D 27
Cow Tower, Norwich—2B 18
Cromer Lifeboat House—1B 10
De Grey Mausoleum, Flitton
—3B 28
Denver Sluice—2C 15
Devil's Dyke, Newmarket—3C 23
Dial House Information Barn,
Brancaster Staithe—1A 8
Dinosaur Natural History Park,
Lenwade—1A 18
Duel Stone, Cawston—3A 10
Duxford Chapel—2B 30
East Anglian Falconry Centre,
Skeyton—3B 10
East of England Birds of Prey &
Conservation Centre,

Laxfield—2C 27
East of England Showground,
Alwalton—3C 13
Essex Showground, Young's
End—2A 40
Fleam Dyke, Fulbourn—1C 31
Fleggburgh Bygone Village, Burgh
St Margaret—1D 19
Flitch Way Visitor Centre,
Rayne—1A 40
Geddington Eleanor Cross
—1A 20
Godwick Deserted Village,
Tittleshall—3C 9
Great War Memorial Column,
Thetford—2A 24
Great Yarmouth House of Wax
—2D 19
Great Yarmouth Merrivale Model
Village—2D 19
Great Yarmouth World of Wax
—2D 19
Hall Farm Equine Rest &
Rehabilitation Centre,
Snetterton—3C 17
Harold's Bridge, Waltham
Abbey—3A 38
Harringworth Viaduct—3A 12
Hatfield Forest, Takeley Street
—1C 39
Hertfordshire Showground,
Redbourn—2B 36
Hethel Old Thorn—2A 18
Hilton Turf Maze—3D 21
Hunstanton Cliffs—1D 7
Isleham Priory Church—2D 23
Ivinghoe Beacon—2A 36
Julian Cell, Norwich—2B 18
Kett's Oak, Wymondham—2A 18
King's College Chapel,
Cambridge—1B 30
Knights Farm, Swan Street
—1B 40
Langham Glass—1D 9
Lexden Earthworks, Colchester
—1C 41
Limekiln, The, Pickworth—1A 12
Lodge Information Centre, The,
Sandy—2C 29
Madingley American Military
Cemetery Memorial Chapel
—1B 30
Millennium Tapestry, Maldon
—3B 40
Mistley Place Park Environmental
& Animal Rescue Centre
Mistley—3A 34
Miton Keynes Bowl—3A 28
Mistley Towers—3A 34

Morston Quay Information
Centre—1D 9
Moulton Packhorse Bridge
—3D 23
Nazing Glass Works,
Broxbourne—3A 38
Nelsons Birthplace, Burnham
Thorpe—1B 8
Nelson's Monument, Great
Yarmouth—2D 19
Norfolk Broads, The—2D 19
Norfolk Shire Horse Centre &
Countryside Collection, West
Runton—1A 10
North Elmham Pound—3C 9
Norwich Civic Regalia,
The Guildhall—2B 18
Ongar Greensted Saxon Wooden
Church, Chipping Ongar
—3C 39
Otter Trust, The, Earsham
—1C 27
Overa House Farm Equine Rest &
Rehabilitation Centre, Larling
—1C 25
Pettitts of Reedham
Feathercraft—2D 19
Pilgrim Fathers Memorial,
Fishtoft—1A 6
Queen's Oak, Huntingfield
—2C 27
Redwings Horse Sanctuary,
Frettenham—1B 18
Royal Norfolk Showground,
Easton—1A 18
R.S.P.B. The Lodge Bird
Sanctuary and Information
Centre, Sandy—2C29
Rutland Water Nature Reserve
Visitor Centre, Manton—2A 12
Saffron Walden Maze—3C 31
St James' Chapel, Rose Green
—2C 33
Shrine of Our Lady of
Walsingham, Little
Walsingham—2C 9
Sizewell Visitor Centre—3D 27
Slipper Chapel & RC Shrine of
Our Lady, Houghton St Giles
—2C 9
Snape Maltings—1C 35
Suffolk Cider Company,
Cretingham—3B 26
Suffolk Showground, Ipswich
—2B 34
Suffolk Water Park, Bramford
—2A 34
Sutton Hoo Archaeological Site,
Woodbridge—2B 34

Tallington Lakes Leisure Park
—2B 12
Taswood Lakes, Tasburgh
—3A 18
Temple Bruer Tower, Welbourn
—1B 4
Thetford Church of The Holy
Sepulchre—1B 24
Thetford Forest Park—3B 16
Tolly Cobbold Brewery, Ipswich
—2A 34
Waltham Cross Eleanor Cross
—3A 38
Wellbank's Orchid World,
Terrington St Clement—1C 15
Wensum Valley Visitor Centre,
North Elmham—3C 9
West Stow Anglo-Saxon Village
—2A 24
Wicksteed Park, Kettering—2A 20
Willow Farm Dried Flower Centre,
Cangate—3C 11
Wing Turf Maze—2A 12
Wood Green Animal Shelter,
Godmanchester —3D 21
Wolterton Park—2A 10
Wroxham Barns, Ashmanhaugh
—3C 11

See also Hill Figure, Hill Fort

Five Knolls Barrows, Dunstable
Downs—1B 36
Grimes Graves, Weeting—1B 24
Robin Hood & Little John
Monoliths, Castor—3C 13
Waulud's Bank, Leagrave—1B 36

Preserved, Steam, Narrow Gauge

Audley End Steam Railway
—3C 31
Barton House Railway,
Wroxham—1C 19
Bure Valley Railway (Broadland
Line), Aylsham—3B 10
Colne Valley Railway, Castle
Hedingham—3A 32
County School Station, North
Elmham—3C 9
East Suffolk Light Railway,
Carlton Colville—3D 19
Great Whipsnade Railway,
Whipsnade Zoo—2B 36
Leighton Buzzard Railway—1A 36
Mangapps Farm Railway
Museum, Burnham-on
-Crouch—3C 41

Nene Valley Railway,
Stibbington—3B 12
North Norfolk Railway (Poppy
Line), Sheringham—1A 10
Pentney Park Railway—1A 16
Rutland Railway, Cottesmore
—1A 12
Wells Harbour Railway, Wells
-next-the-Sea—1C 9
Wells & Walsingham Light
Railway, Wells-next-the-Sea
—1C 9

Barnack Hills & Holes—2B 12
Burgh Castle—2D 19
Caister Roman Site, Caister-on
-Sea—1D 19
Reach Roman Remains—3C 23
St Albans Roman Wall—3C 37
Verulamium Roman Theatre, St
Albans—3C 37
Welwyn Roman Baths—2D 37

Pleasurewood Hills American
Theme Park, Corton—3D 19

OPEN ALL YEAR
*Note: Telephone Numbers are
given in Italics*

Ampthill Tourist Information
Centre—3B 28
01525 402051 EXT 360
Bedford Tourist Information
Centre—2B 28
01234 215226
Berkhamsted Tourist Information
Centre—3A 36
01442 877638
Bishop's Stortford Tourist
Information Centre—1B 38
01279 652274
Borehamwood Tourist Information
Centre—3C 37
0181 207 7496
Boston Tourist Information
Centre—1A 6
01205 356656
Braintree Tourist Information
Centre—1A 40
01376 550066
Bury St Edmunds Tourist
Information Centre—3B 24
01284 764667

Cambridge Tourist Information
  Centre—1B 30
  01223 322640
Chelmsford Tourist Information
  Centre—3A 40
  01245 283400
Clacton-on-Sea Tourist
  Information Centre—2A 42
  01255 423400
Colchester Tourist Information
  Centre—1C 41
  01206 282920
Corby Tourist Information
  Centre—1A 20
  01536 407507
Cromer Tourist Information
  Centre—1B 10
  01263 512497
Diss Tourist Information Centre
  —2A 26
  01379 650523
Downham Market Tourist
  Information Centre—2D 15
  01366 387440
Dunstable Tourist Information
  Centre—1B 36
  01582 471012
Ely Tourist Information Centre
  —1C 23
  01353 662062
Felixstowe Tourist Information
  Centre—3B 34
  01394 276770
Grantham Tourist Information
  Centre—2A 4
  01476 66444
Great Yarmouth Tourist
  Information Centre (Town
  Hall)—2D 19   *01493 846345*
Hadleigh Tourist Information
  Centre—2D 33
  01473 823824
Harwich Tourist Information
  Centre, Parkeston—3B 34
  01255 506139
Hemel Hempstead Tourist
  Information Centre—3B 36
  01442 234222
Hertford Tourist Information
  Centre—2A 38
  01992 584322
Hitchin Tourist Information
  Centre—1C 37
  01462 434738/450133
Hunstanton Tourist Information
  Centre—1D 7
  01485 532610
Huntingdon Tourist Information
  Centre—2D 21

01480 388588
Ipswich Tourist Information
  Centre—2A 34
  01473 258070
Kettering Tourist Information
  Centre—2A 20
  01536 410266 / 410333
King's Lynn Tourist Information
  Centre—1D 15
  01553 763044
Lowestoft Tourist Information
  Centre—3D 19
  01502 523000
Luton Tourist Information
  Centre—1B 36
  01582 401579
Maldon Tourist Information
  Centre—3B 40
  01621 856503
Milton Keynes Tourist Information
  Centre—3A 28
  01908 232525 / 231742
Newmarket Tourist Information
  Centre—3D 23
  01638 667200
Norwich Tourist Information
  Centre—2B 18
  01603 666071
Oakham Tourist Information
  Centre—2A 12
  01572 724329
Oundle Tourist Information
  Centre—1B 20
  01832 274333
Peterborough Tourist Information
  Centre—3C 13
  01733 317336
Saffron Walden Tourist
  Information Centre—3C 31
  01799 510444
St Albans Tourist Information
  Centre—3C 37
  01727 864511
Sleaford Tourist Information
  Centre—1B 4
  01529 414294
South Mimms Services Tourist
  Information Centre—3D 37
  01707 643233
Spalding Tourist Information
  Centre—3D 5
  01775 725468 / 761161
Stamford Tourist Information
  Centre—2B 12
  01780 55611
Stevenage Tourist Information
  Centre—1D 37
  01438 369441
Stowmarket Tourist Information

Centre—1D 33
  01449 676800
Thetford Tourist Information
  Centre—1B 24
  01842 752599
Wellingborough Tourist
  Information Centre—3A 20
  01933 228101
Welwyn Garden City Tourist
  Information Centre—2D 37
  01707 390653 / 339211
Wendover Tourist Information
  Centre—3A 36
  01296 696759
Wisbech Tourist Information
  Centre—2B 14
  01945 583263

OPEN SUMMER SEASON ONLY

Aldeburgh Tourist Information
  Centre—1D 35
  01728 453637
Aylsham Tourist Information
  Centre—3A 10
  01263 733903
Beccles Tourist Information
  Centre—3D 19
  01502 713196
Cranwell Tourist Information
  Centre, North Rauceby—1B 4
  01529 488490
Fakenham Tourist Information
  Centre—3C 9
  01328 851981
Great Yarmouth Tourist
  Information Centre (Marine
  Parade)—2D 19
  01493 842195
Hoveton Tourist Information
  Centre—1C 19
  01603 782281
Lavenham Tourist Information
  Centre—2C 33
  01787 248207
Mundesley Tourist Information
  Centre—2C 11
  01263 721070
Ranworth Tourist Information
  Centre—1C 19
  01603 270453
Rutland Water Tourist Information
  Centre, Empingham—2A 12
  01780 460321
Sheringham Tourist Information
  Centre—1A 10
  01263 824329
Southwold Tourist Information
  Centre—2D 27
  01502 724729

Sudbury Tourist Information Centre—2B 32
01787 881320
Swaffham Tourist Information Centre—2B 16
01760 722255
Walsingham Tourist Information Centre, Little Walsingham —2C 9   01328 820510
Walton-on-the-Naze Tourist Information Centre—1B 42
01255 675542
Watton Tourist Information Centre—2C 17
01953 882058 / 884224
Wells-next-the-Sea Tourist Information Centre—1C 9
01328 710885
Woburn Tourist Information Centre—3A 28
01525 290631

Vineyard

Boyton Vineyards, Boyton End —2A 32
Bruisyard Vineyard & Winery —3C 27
Chilford Hundred Vineyard, Linton—2C 31
Felsted Vineyard, Bartholomew Green—1A 40
Gifford's Hall Vineyard, Hartest —1B 32
Manor Vineyards, Cavendish —2B 32
New Hall Vineyard, Rudley Green—3B 40
Priory Vineyards, Little Dunmow —1D 39
Shawsgate Vineyard & Winery, Brabling Green—3B 26

Wildlife Park

See also Farm Park, Bird Garden, Zoo

Hamerton Wildlife Centre—1C 21

Mole Hall Wildlife Park, Widdington—3C 31
Norfolk Wildlife Park, Sparhamhill—1D 17
Paradise Wildlife Park, Broxbourne—3A 38
Suffolk Wildlife & Rare Breeds Park, Kessingland—1D 27
Thrigby Hall Wildlife Gardens —1D 19
Willers Mill Wildlife Park & Sanctuary, Shepreth—2A 30

Windmill

Aythorpe Roding Postmill, Roundbush Green—2C 39
Bardwell Towermill—2C 25
Berney Arms `High Mill' Windpump, Halvergate Marshes—2D 19
Billingford Towermill—2A 26
Boardman's Trestle Windpump, How Hill—1C 19
Bocking Postmill, Bocking Churchstreet—1A 40
Boston `Maud Foster' Towermill —1A 6
Bourn Postmill, Caxton—1A 30
Burwell `Stevens' Towermill —3C 23
Buttrum's Towermill, Woodbridge—2B 34
Clayrack Windpump, How Hill —1C 19
Cley Towermill, Cley next the Sea—1D 9
Cromer Postmill—1A 38
Dereham Towermill—1D 17
Eastry Windpump, Stowmarket —1D 33
Fulbourn Smockmill—1C 31
Great Bircham Towermill—2A 8
Great Chishill Postmill—3B 30
Great Gransden Postmill—1D 29
Heckington Towermill—1C 5
Herringfleet Smock Windpump —3D 19

Horsey Windpump—3D 11
Ingleborough (West Walton) Towermill—1B 14
Little Cressingham Wind & Watermill—2B 16
Mountnessing Postmill—3D 39
Pitstone Green Postmill—2A 36
St Olaves's Trestle Windpump —3D 19
Saxtead Green Postmill—3B 26
Sibsey 'Trader' Towermill—1A 6
Soham 'Downfield' Towermill —2D 23
Soham 'Shade' Smockmill —2C 23
Stansted Mountfitchet Towermill —1C 39
Starston Windpump—1B 26
Stevington Postmill—1A 28
Stock Towermill—3D 39
Stow Towermill, Paston—2C 11
Stracey Arms Windpump, Halvergate Marshes—2D 19
Sutton Towermill—3C 11
Thaxted `John Webb's' Towermill—3D 31
Thelnetham Towermill—2D 25
Thorpeness Hollow Post Windpump—1D 35
Thurne Dyke Windpump—1D 19
Wicken Fen Windpump—2C 23
Wicklewood Towermill—2D 17
Wymondham Towermill—1A 12

Zoo / Safari Park

See also Bird Garden, Farm Park, Wildlife Park

Banham Zoo & Monkey Sanctuary—1D 25
Colchester Zoo, Heckfordbridge —1C 41
Linton Zoo—2C 31
Whipsnade Zoo/ Wild Animal Park—2B 36
Woburn Wild Animal Kingdom —3A 28